"Banjo" Paterson's
HIGH COUNTRY

"Banjo" Paterson's
HIGH COUNTRY

TIM HALL   PHOTOGRAPHY TRISHA DIXON

*CORNSTALK PUBLISHING
An imprint of CollinsAngus&Robertson Publishers Pty Limited*

*First published in Australia by Angus & Robertson Publishers in 1989
This Cornstalk edition published in 1992 by
CollinsAngus&Robertson Publishers Pty Limited (ACN 009 913 517)
A division of HarperCollinsPublishers (Australia) Pty Limited
25–31 Ryde Road, Pymble NSW 2073, Australia*

*HarperCollinsPublishers (New Zealand) Limited
31 View Road, Glenfield, Auckland 10, New Zealand*

*HarperCollinsPublishers Limited
77– 85 Fulham Palace Road, London W6 8JB, United Kingdom*

*National Library of Australia
Cataloguing-in-Publication data:*

*Hall, Timothy, 1938–
    Banjo Paterson's high country.*

*Includes indez.
ISBN 0 207 15754 5*

*1. Paterson, A. B. (Andrew Barton), 1864–1941 – Settings.
2. Snowy Mountains (N. S. W.) in literature.
3. Monaro (N. S. W.) – in literature.
4. Snowy Mountains (N. S. W.) – History.
5. Monaro (N. S. W.) – History.
I. Dixon, Trisha, 1953–
II. Paterson, A. B. (Andrew Barton), 1864–1941.
III. Title. IV. Title: High country.*

A821'.2

*Typeset in 10/13pt Baskerville by Midland Typesetters, Victoria
Printed in Hong Kong*

*5 4 3 2
95 94 93 92*

Contents

Introduction

Of all the images of their country that Australians cling to, few are more evocative than that of the high country and the legendary men of the Snowy Mountains galloping in reckless pursuit of wild horses, stockwhip in hand over "snow-covered icy precipices where every step promises instant disaster for man and horse falling down to some dark abyss far below".

It was the special genius of "Banjo" Paterson — his real name was Andrew Barton Paterson — that he could bring this beautiful part of Australia and the exploits of these men to life in his writing; and no poem has captured so vividly the very soul of the high country, at once magnificent and lonely, and sometimes very frightening, as *The Man from Snowy River.*

It is an immensely satisfying poem, set against the wilderness and beauty of these desolate mountains, slashed by steep-sided ravines "that in the parting of the day, when black shadows fall on inky blackness, seem bottomless", and the stage is set for one of the great pursuits of literature. There could be no better place to begin a journey into Banjo Paterson's high country.

Banjo Paterson: bush balladeer

The Man from Snowy River was published in the Sydney *Bulletin* on 26 April 1890, under Paterson's pseudonym, "The Banjo", a name that he took from a station racehorse owned by his family. It was a time for pseudonyms and he wrote under at least six others. Not until five years later did the poem appear in a book, *The Man from Snowy River and Other Verses*, which was an immediate success. It sold out in its first week and can rightly claim to have been Australia's first genuine best–seller.

Almost a hundred years later, it is not easy to put into proper perspective the importance of the bush ballad then, in the daily lives of the men and women who lived there. They had no entertainment but the entertainment they made for themselves, and from one corner of the continent to the other, they learned their favourite ballads by heart and told them over and over again round their camp fires or in their huts when the long nights drew in and they huddled inside to keep out the cold.

The 1890s were years when there were scores of ballad writers in Australia, and nowhere did they receive more encouragement than in the pages of J. F. Archibald's *Bulletin*. The two most celebrated balladeers were Paterson and Henry Lawson, and they have always been compared, not always favourably for Paterson when their skill as poets has been placed on the scale. Considering how they dominated the same scene, it is remarkable how unalike the two men were: they could hardly have approached their subjects from more different backgrounds.

Paterson was an uncomplicated man, a devoted father and husband, who was well born, well travelled and self-effacing. He had been encouraged to write poetry by his grandmother, herself a talented poet, and he enjoyed, as his biographer Clement Semmler put it, "a homely, hearty humour, open as daylight". The poet and critic Douglas Stewart said of him that "he lifted the settled gloom from our literature of the bush". His nature was indeed to be optimistic, but he could turn on the pathos with the best of them when he thought it was called for:

> And the mother kept feebly calling, with a hope that wouldn't die,
> "Willie! Where are you, Willie?" But how can the dead reply?

Lawson, the younger by three years, was born in a tent on a gold claim and had little formal education, unlike Paterson who was a successful solicitor. Paterson, in spite of a few upsets, never had to carry Lawson's burden of constant debt, deafness (he was totally deaf from

Banjo Paterson loved the bush and based many of his poems on people he had met there and tales they told. Today, a new generation of bushmen caretakes the high country, and it is men such as Bill Hicks (opposite) and Jim Commins (above) who carry on the traditions handed down by their forebears.

the age of fourteen), alcoholism and depressing stints in gaol for failing to maintain his wife.

But if their perspectives were necessarily different, it is quite wrong to assume, as some have done, that Paterson's concern for the underdog was any less sincere than Lawson's, or indeed that he was any less radical. Lawson experienced poverty at first hand, but Paterson was no less disturbed by what he saw as a solicitor. He practised for ten years, but then grew disenchanted with life in the city and hankered to be back in the bush. His poem *Clancy of the Overflow* was a plea to be freed from his city desk.

> *I was sitting in my dingy little office, where a stingy*
> *Ray of sunlight struggles feebly down between the houses*
> *   tall,*
> *And the foetid air and gritty of the dusty, dirty city*
> *Through the open window floating, spreads its foulness*
> *   over all.*
>
> *And in place of lowing cattle, I can hear the fiendish*
> *   rattle*
> *Of the tramways and the buses making hurry down the*
> *   street,*
> *And the language uninviting of the gutter children*
> *   fighting,*
> *Comes fitfully and faintly through the ceaseless tramp of*
> *   feet.*
>
> *And the hurrying people daunt me, and their pallid faces*
> *   haunt me*
> *As they shoulder one another in their rush and nervous*
> *   haste,*
> *With their eager eyes and greedy, and their stunted forms*
> *   and weedy,*
> *For townsfolk have no time to grow, they have no time to*
> *   waste.*
>
> *And I somehow rather fancy that I'd like to change with*
> *   Clancy,*
> *Like to take a turn at droving where the seasons come and*
> *   go,*
> *While he faced the round eternal of the cashbook and the*
> *   journal—*
> *But I doubt he'd suit the office, Clancy of "The*
> *   Overflow".*

Banjo Paterson: bush balladeer

Most of the controversy that is supposed to have existed between Paterson and Lawson was concocted by the two of them. In fact they got along well and were friends, but they liked the idea of a fictitious bush controversy, and thought it would do their writing careers no harm.

> *You had better stick to Sydney and make merry with the*
> *"Push",*
> *For the bush will never suit you, and you'll never suit the*
> *bush,*

Paterson wrote in an open letter to Lawson, who had come back from the bush swearing that he would stay in town until the bush was civilised.

It comes as something of a surprise, when one sees how superbly Paterson describes the high country of south-eastern Australia, and how deeply he felt for it, that in all his prolific writing, he wrote about it no more than half a dozen times. It was mainly the bush of the outback that he wrote about, of little people coping with drought and flies and heat and dust in the west. Yet what he wrote about the high country was among his best work. The delightful *Geebung Polo Club,* for example, was based on the real Cooma Polo Club for which he appears to have played. Its players were "demons with mighty little science and a mighty lot of dash", who are still remembered with awe for leaving the ground looking more like a battle-field than a sports arena after their matches.

Paterson knew, too, the respect, even fear, that many horsemen from outside the mountains held for those bleak forbidding hills of the high country. Every year, many of these men had to take their stock up into the mountains to graze, and Paterson wrote a poem, *The Mountain Squatter,* about the way they waited for those unwelcome trips.

> *These Riverina cracks,*   *Their horses shake with fear,*
> *They do not care to ride*   *When loosened boulders go,*
> *The half-inch*   *With leaps,*
>   *hanging tracks*   *like startled deer,*
> *Along the mountain side.*   *Down the gulfs below.*

Paterson was not the first popular author to write of the forbidding mountains. Nine years earlier, Rolf Boldrewood (the pseudonym of Thomas Alexander Browne, a police

magistrate), had written his classic tale of villainy *Robbery Under Arms.* In it the cattle duffing Marston family drive their mob through the mountains on the way to sell them in Victoria. They stop at Terrible Hollow, a secret valley where they could hide up safely with the entire mob. Dick Marston walks to the edge of the mountain and looks over. "It was like the end of the world. Far down, there was a dark, dreadful drop into a sort of deep valley below. You couldn't see the bottom of it. The trees on the mountainside looked like bushes and they were big ironbarks and messmates, too. On three sides of us was this awful, desolate-looking precipice—a dreary, gloomy, God-forsaken kind of spot."

Paterson would almost certainly have read and related to Boldrewood's description for when he came to write about the mountains himself, he saw them in the same light.

> *Then fast the horsemen followed, there the gorges deep*
>   *and black,*
> *Resounded to the thunder of their tread,*
> *And the stockwhips woke the echoes, and they fiercely*
>   *answered back*
> *From cliffs and crags that beetled overhead.*

Paterson's genius was that *The Man from Snowy River* is equally satisfying to those who have never seen a wild horse, never heard the crack of a stockwhip echoing through the valleys and ravines, never known the fear of staring down into the black ravines, as it is to the mountain people themselves.

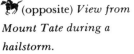

(opposite) View from Mount Tate during a hailstorm.

(left) John Fitzgerald rides through the mist near Kelly's yards, on his way to the Bogong High Plains.

Banjo Paterson.

3

Banjo Paterson: bush balladeer

The poem passed the acid test of being accepted as the work of a man who understood and felt for those who lived in the mountains and the high country, with all their tribulations and not very frequent pleasures. But most telling of all, even a hundred years later, the descendants of those people still vie for the right to claim the original "Man from Snowy River" in their families.

Paterson himself always insisted that he had not been writing about any particular man. "The verses were intended as a ballad, not as a newspaper report of a sporting event," he wrote to one group who wanted to put up a memorial to their favourite, describing him on it as "The Man from Snowy River". And to a Light Horse sergeant in Egypt during World War I (Paterson served there with a remount unit), a man who came from the mountains, he insisted, "He was in the category of Rolf Boldrewood's Captain Starlight, a brainchild of my own imagination".

That is as may be, but Paterson was certainly not short of models on which to base his hero. He was an excellent journalist who knew the bush well and was trusted and respected by the people he met in the high country. He loved nothing more than to sit round their camp fires, listening to their stories, keeping meticulous notes of all he heard.

In a memoir, *Looking Backward*, Paterson said that he had actually been writing about cleaning up the wild horses around his own property near Yass (which must have meant the property where he lived as a child, Illalong, for it was not until eighteen years after he wrote *The Man from Snowy River* that he bought Coodra Vale at Wee Jasper, midway between Yass and Tumut). "To make a job of it, I had to create a character, to imagine a man who would ride better than anybody else, and where would he come from except the Snowy? And what sort of horse would he ride, except a half-thoroughbred mountain pony?"

He said, a little disingenuously for he knew very well that it was the case, "I felt convinced that there must have been a 'Man from Snowy River'. I was right. They turned up from all the mountain districts—men who did exactly the same ride and could give you chapter and verse for every hill they descended and every creek they crossed".

Paterson said of his legendary Man, "I felt convinced that there must have been a Man from Snowy River. I was right. They turned up from all the mountain districts—men who did exactly the same ride and could give you chapter and verse for every hill they descended and every creek they crossed". The legend lives on.

In search of The Man

Knowing the exploits of some of the men whose stories Paterson had heard before he wrote the poem, it is possible to piece together a pastiche of the most likely sources that he used for the man who hailed from Snowy River, up by Kosciusko's side.

There were some, on the fringes of immortality, whose reputations rested rather uncertainly on their ability to stay on a horse no matter what. Some did it sober, like Hell Fire Jack Clarke; a great many more would do it while trying to ride down vertical cliffs after a few drinks. But *The Man from Snowy River* is about much more than a man who could ride down a steep mountain without falling off.

It is about a very ordinary man, a mere stripling, who came from nowhere, snatched victory from certain failure, and proved the pundits wrong. Paterson, like Lawson, excelled at what Archibald called "howling for the undermost dog".

Jim Troy was an underdog. He lived out of Wagga Wagga and when his brother-in-law, Tom Macnamara, announced that he was going out to bring in three good horses that had broken away and joined the brumbies in the hills near Tumut, Jim was the first to say that he was going with him. But his elder brother, Tom Troy, laughed, because Jim was so young and his horse so puny.

But still so slight and weary, one would doubt his power to stay,
And the old man said, 'That horse will never do
For a long and tiring gallop—lad, you'd better stop away,
Those hills are far too rough for such as you'.

But Tom Macnamara looked at the boy and at his horse and said firmly that they should be allowed to go too.

So he waited sad and wistful—only Clancy stood his friend—
'I think we ought to let him come,' he said;
'I warrant he'll be with us when he's wanted at the end,
For both his horse and he are mountain bred'.

Jim Troy didn't disgrace himself and years later, but before the poem was written, Tom Macnamara and some of his friends were telling the tale round a camp fire and Paterson was among the men there, writing it all down in his notebook.

Today's stockmen of the high country, Robert Ward (opposite) *and Ken Connley* (above).

He seemed to like the idea of bringing Clancy into *The Man from Snowy River*.

And Clancy of the Overflow came down to lend a hand,
No better horseman ever held the reins;
For never horse would throw him while the saddle girths
    would stand,
He learnt to ride while droving on the plains.

Another popular contender was Lachlan Cochran, from Yaouk near Adaminaby. A fearless buckjump rider and jockey, he had come back from the Boer War in South Africa with five medals, and his skill and courage in the saddle were the subject of numerous stories that Paterson might well have heard.

Lachlan's brother Neil turned out to be a match for his brother. He received a telegram one day to say that Lachlan was dying in hospital in Cootamundra and wanted to see him before he went. There was a train departing from Tumut the next morning which, with luck, would get him to the hospital in time: the only problem was that Tumut was 130 kilometres away, and the journey lay over some of the steepest and most treacherous country in the mountains— by night.

Neil did not leve Yaouk until nearly dusk. Like many of the old mountain people, he had an extraordinary sixth sense that enabled him to navigate unerringly even in the darkness and the fog. He had covered more than 110 kilometres in thirteen hours, when his horse broke down as they went down the hill into Blowering. Neil changed the horse at a station he was passing, and on a borrowed mare rode on towards Tumut. He arrived an hour later at a fast canter, as the train's whistle was sounding mournfully over the town, and he reached Cootamundra just in time to see his brother before he slipped into a coma and died. A local poet wrote some lines about Neil that include the verse

Then out to Adaminaby, the word was quickly sped,
Of a horseman who was dying far away.
He was longing for a message from his kinsfold
mountain-bred
To bring the mountain air where he lay.

Just before he died, Macnamara recalled, "I well remember the ride as if it took place yesterday. From Troy's place, you could see the hills in the direction of Tumut. Our adventure was not down Kosciusko side, as Paterson was saying. Banjo shifted the mountain into our country to make the poem poetic".

It is little wonder that their families still insist that Tom Macnamara was "Clancy" and young Jim Troy the "Man" himself. Clancy, incidentally, was a name that Paterson seemed to find appealing for he used it more than once, most memorably in *Clancy of the Overflow* which is generally considered, with *The Man from Snowy River* and *Waltzing Matilda,* to be one of his three best poems.

Paterson himself described how as a solicitor he wrote "to a gentleman in the bush who had not paid his debts". The memorable reply came back, from a friend of the gentleman, "Clancy's gone to Queensland droving, and we don't know where he are". Paterson included the words, unaltered, in *Clancy of the Overflow.*

John Clancy was real enough, though his family insisted that he never went nearer the Snowy Mountains than Dubbo on the western plains of New South Wales. He was a wild Irish drover, working on a sheep station called Overflow, 130 kilometres north-west of Condobolin in the west of New South Wales.

8

(opposite, top) Riders from all over the mountains travel to Lake Jillamatong near Moonbah each year for the Mountain Muster. The traditions of generations are carried on by Milton Golby from Ingebyra (opposite, below) and Lisa and Gary Caldwell from Moonbah (left).

James Spencer was another man who had a strong claim. Paterson sent him an autographed copy of the book and stayed with him at the house at Waste Point that Spencer had built for himself at the junction of the Snowy and the Thredbo Rivers.

In the 1840s, Spencer had rented Mount Kosciusko as a 10,500 hectare cattle run, and named it Excelsior Station. He abandoned it a few years later because the grazing season was too short. "A man is fortunate if he can keep his stock more than three months on it," he complained.

Spencer was a big, burly, kindly bushman, whose fame as a horseman was so widespread in the high country that Paterson would have been almost bound to have heard of it in his travels round the mountains. He had a reputation for riding after cattle, no matter how rough or steep the country, and he would set off on a long chase after a wild horse, just for the fun of it, and then let it go.

After he gave up Excelsior, he became a much sought-after guide and he acted as guide to the botanist and explorer, Ferdinand von Mueller in 1851, when von Mueller climbed and measured the height of all the major peaks in the Kosciusko range.

The most convincing claimant, however, to have been the elusive model for *The Man from Snowy River*, and the man whom Paterson himself said had most influenced him, was a wiry little Irishman, barely 155 centimetres tall, called Jack Riley. Riley came to Australia when he was fifteen, served time for horse stealing, and like so many of his countrymen, was an expert horseman. He had a reputation as a fearless rider and stockman.

If he sighted cattle or a horse that he wanted to chase, no matter how hard the country, he would characteristically pull his hat down over his ears, dig in his heels and be off!

For nearly thirty years Riley lived and worked at Tom Groggin station, straddling the Victorian and New South Wales border, which he dummied for the real owner 112 kilometres away at Greg Greg station. Dummying involved buying land ostensibly for oneself, but in reality for someone else. It was commonly done and it was usually necessary. Selectors were only allowed a small portion of land, which was not sufficient for a stock run to be economically viable.

Tom Groggin—the name came from the Aboriginal "ton-a-roggin", meaning the place of many water spiders—belonged to a man called Pearce, who ran young horses along with his cattle. He kept his horses there until they were three and a half years old, when they were brought in and fattened up for the Indian market. Horses couldn't be imported into India until they were four, because the climate took too heavy a toll on them.

These horses inevitably attracted the brumbies which came down to a safe distance outside the paddocks and the yards and tried to lure them away. They were often successful and there was one particular horse, a beautiful grey-white gelding, three-parts thoroughbred, which ran off and which Riley could never catch. It was as cunning and canny a horse as ever he saw running in the mountains and to recapture it became almost an obsession with him.

For eighteen months the gelding eluded him. In summer it went far up above the winter snow-line to feed on the snow grass, and in winter it came down, but always stayed

There were many claimants to the title of the Man from Snowy River. ". . . a man who would ride better than anybody else, and where else would he come from except from the Snowy?"

well away from the area where it seemed to know instinctively that Riley was running and trapping wild horses.

After a year and a half of this, Riley was determined that he wasn't going to be outwitted. He built a yard on the Leather Barrel, across a trail that he knew the horse was using, but left each end open to allay its suspicions until more men came up from Greg Greg to help him.

The wild horse's speed and eyesight alone make it more than a match for most men on horseback in a straight race. The horse's instinct, when it is startled, is to head for the safety of the range, always making for the most inaccessible places. In these situations, it is the reaction of the saddle horse, not its rider, that will save them. One of the first lessons that a young brumby runner must learn is to give his horse its head!

The stockmen must try to cut the brumbies off and keep them in open country. The aim of most runs is to steady the mob and drive it into a trap yard like the one that Jack Riley built on Leather Barrel. The yards have long wings, or Vs, running for up to five kilometres into the bush, getting progressively wider as they go. The horses are driven into the widest part of this funnel and are then kept inside the wings, which used to be made from strips of calico strung from tree to tree, with paper hanging from them.

If the horses can be kept moving hard and straight, they are likely to stay within the wings until it is too late to escape; but the moment anything panics them, they might wheel and break through the calico. Nothing will then induce them to come anywhere near those wings again.

Along the length of the wings, the men wait in silence, the suspense electrifying. It is always their horses that are first to sense that the brumbies are coming. Their ears prick and they begin to fidget like war horses picking up the sound of the distant bugle. Their heads move constantly, straining for the first sight of the mob, while their riders curse them softly and urge them to silence. Horses' eyes do not have variable focus like humans', and objects at different distances register only on different parts of the retina. They must tilt their heads continuously to keep things in focus.

And then suddenly, almost without warning, the mob is on top of them, crashing through the undergrowth and the trees, hooves flying over the ground, drawing sparks from the flintstone. The noise is deafening. Adrenalin pumping furiously, the riders fall into place silently beside the mob. There must be no raised voices, no exaggerated movements.

If it is done carefully, the wild horses often do not seem to sense at first that the men are there. Keep them going hard and straight, is the rule. But that can change in a moment, and seemingly as one the realisation comes to them that they have been tricked. Their ears go flat and there is a fearful whinnying and snorting as they sense that they are trapped and try to wheel and break out of the wings. If the men are not up to the job, this is the moment when the horses will break away and head for the slopes and certain freedom.

Banjo Paterson wrote an essay on yarding wild horses which was never published in his life time. It describes vividly the last stages of a brumby run, when the horses are beginning to tire and the men sense victory.

After a few miles, the weaker horses in the wild mob, the mares and foals and so on, begin to drop out. These strike off by themselves, cantering or trotting slowly while the main body sweeps on. As the pace begins to tell, more and more drop out, some quite exhausted; these stand still and come in for a savage cut or two of the whip as the pursuers come by. The others keep going, the gallop at length dropping to a swaying canter and then to a trot.

By this time, the stock horses are in a pitiable condition, bloody with spurring, and hardly able to raise a canter; some will have been crippled by the rough country, and others will have knocked up altogether and dropped out of the running.

Then comes the final charge of the mob, when they raise a staggering canter to make for some particular

point, and the stockmen, plying whip and spur, manage to head them off, and the mob, beaten and downcast, jogs sullenly along.

Any horse without a brand is fair game, even the unbranded foal running beside its branded mother. And even if there is a brand, who bothers to ask questions?

Jack Riley had built his wings far into the bush. He took the bottom position for himself, nearest the yard, because he knew that this was where the grey would almost certainly break away if it was going to, and he wanted to be ready to follow. At the far end of the wings, the other men had drawn a half circle, and brought the horse down slowly. It was even trickier when there was only one animal and there was none of the momentum generated by a mob which kept the horses running together, at least for a while.

The gelding knew that something was wrong. It was skittish and whistling and suspicious of every move. Riley heard it coming before he saw it. Then it was in sight, a magnificent animal, even after eighteen months in the bush and with its coat matted and torn. He watched it come slowly down, well aware that the horse knew he was there. Then suddenly it broke.

Instead of going into the yard, just metres away, it galloped straight down the sheer mountainside that was all hop and scrub and mountain ash. It was so steep that Riley had felt sure when he positioned the yard, that it would break the other way. In a flash, he pulled down his hat, dug in his spurs and was off in pursuit.

The others, sitting on their horses, could hear the clattering and squealing all the way down the mountain, getting further and further away until they were sure that both horses, and Jack Riley with them, had made their last run. But then came another noise, less frantic this time, and as they watched, first the head and then the body of the grey came over the crest of the hill and close behind it, Jack Riley. It was completely blown, and as it reached the track, it went gently into the yard and the men slipped the panel behind it.

Riley told how he had stayed close to the grey right to the foot of the mountain, travelling so fast that the tears in his eyes had blinded him. The steep descent and then a fast chase down the valley seemed to tell the gelding that

(top) *Kosciusko National Park stockman.* (above) *Nimmitabel cattleman, Bill Herbert.*

(top right) *Glen Symons from Moonbah.* (bottom right) *John and Barry Fitzgerald on the Bogong high plains.*

at last it had met its match. Riley somehow got in front of it and cut it off, heading it back towards the place where they had come down and suddenly all the spirit went out of his quarry and the chase was over.

For a long time, the story of Jack Riley bringing home his grey was told around the fires, probably stretched a little here, embellished there. Paterson spent a night with Riley, bringing with him a bottle of whisky, which Riley liked "little and often". Paterson said later to a friend that it was listening to Riley relating his adventures that gave him the idea of writing *The Man from Snowy River*.

Jack Riley's last days were fitting for this old mountain legend. Even when he was eighty, he refused to leave his mountain home—a slab hut that he had built and where he lived alone—except for rare visits to Corryong, 90 kilometres away, with his packhorses to replenish his supplies.

Early in 1914, however, his condition—he had dropsy—became serious and a party of men, concerned about him, went up to Tom Groggin and found him in bed, seriously ill. They had to get him out, grumbling and unco-operative, and into the little cottage hospital at Corryong, but the Murray was in flood so that it was impossible to ford it and take him by the direct route. Instead, they went round by way of Hermit's Hill on a goat track, covering most of the journey with one of them sitting on Riley's horse behind him to hold him on.

A heavy snowstorm came down, but Riley insisted on riding to the top of Hermit's Hill which is a steep pinch. They made the ascent with great difficulty. It was to be his last ride, as well he knew. That night they camped in a hut at Surveyor's Creek, with a blizzard howling outside, and the next day they finished the journey with the old Irishman barely conscious.

Just before he died, Riley called for a priest to administer the last rites. When he got there, the father found Riley clearly disturbed about something. "Father, Banjo's got this wrong!" he kept insisting. "That's not the mountain he's got in the poem, not the mountain I told him. He shouldn't have gone and changed it around. That wasn't right."

Later, they erected a headstone on his grave in the Corryong graveyard and put on it the words, "In Memory of the Man from Snowy River".

Wild horses: Brumby's legacy

There have been wild horses in the high country almost since the first days of white settlement and they have become an inseparable part of the folklore of the mountains. To come by chance on a mob of brumbies on a winter's morning before the mist has lifted is an unforgettable experience. Half hidden in the trees, they seem to merge into the shadows, the occasional grey among them ghostly in the mountain fog, barely visible against the still crisp snow.

Then, in an instant, the spell is broken. A snapping twig, a warning scent on the still, chill morning air, and as one the mob prick their ears, turn towards the intruder, then wheel away. They run so close together that daylight barely separates them, hooves drumming over the frozen ground, clattering on the loose rocks.

The purists would claim that they are not truly wild at all, that they are all descended from domesticated animals, either turned loose or lured from their paddocks by a free-roaming mob. And in a sense they are right. There were no horses in Australia before white settlement, but to argue beyond this that Australia's brumbies are somehow less than wild, is to have no knowledge of their nature, for they are as wild as any creature in the mountains.

Almost no other domesticated animal adapts to the wild with as much facility as the horse and it takes only five generations for the descendants of even the most blue-blooded thoroughbred runaway to revert to creatures that in appearance and behaviour are indistinguishable from brumbies that have been interbreeding for a century and more.

Many of the wild horses on the Victorian side of the mountains can indeed trace their ancestry back that far, to a mob that belonged to an old pioneer at Suggan Buggan, David O'Rourke, who died in the middle of the last century. O'Rourke left no will, and no heir came forward to claim his estate or his numerous stockhorses. As they were almost worthless when he died, no one even bothered to muster them out in the paddocks and to save the cost of feed they were turned loose.

The same thing happened on the other side of the mountains at about the same time. Many of the horses on the 14 Monaro properties of the entrepreneur Ben Boyd were let loose after Boyd's extraordinary empire collapsed. Boyd had controlled 890,000 hectares and owned hundreds of horses. Many more were imported during the mid-nineteenth century gold rushes and were freed when the rush petered out. Others again were freed by the nineteenth century equivalent of today's joyriders. Shearers and itinerants tramping across country on foot would sometimes help themselves to a quiet horse they encountered in a paddock and turn it loose when they

Many of the wild horses in the Victorian border country can trace their ancestry back to a mob of horses belonging to Suggan Buggan pioneer David O'Rourke. After his death the horses were let loose in the mountains and joined the brumby herds.

15

The wild horses manage to cope with most types of weather, but high country names such as Dead Horse Gap bear witness to their occasional fallibility.

reached their destination. And many more simply escaped, seduced into the wild by a whinnying mob of brumbies calling to them over the paddock fence.

There are several stories to explain how the word brumby came into the language. As good as any is the story told about a Major Brumby, who was transferred from New South Wales to Tasmania in 1904. The horses he left behind at Richmond Hill were allowed to run free because nobody wanted them. "Whose horses are those?" the dealers asked, and they were told, "They're Brumby's". It was the horse dealers who coined the word and used it at the saleyards, until brumbies became the generic word for Australia's wild horses. In the high country, however, they spurned the word and went on calling them wild horses for generations. Many still do.

The brumbies are far removed from the sleek, well-fed, ring-ins that play their roles in modern movies. Rarely more than fifteen hands high, they are scrawny, thin-boned animals after generations of in-breeding. At the time when Paterson was writing, however, the horses' bloodline was much better; far more care went into breeding good stockhorses and there were many more of them. Inevitably, a good number escaped and they put new blood into animals that otherwise would grow progressively weaker from continual in-breeding—"giving them back bone", is how the mountain men put it.

Brood mares in particular strengthened the blood line of the brumbies. No mob carries more than one stallion, but mares will find a home without difficulty. More recently, in 1940, Herbie Hain, one of the best packhorse trainers the mountains have seen, released 175 mares as there was no food for them lower down. They included an assortment of animals, from draught horses to ponies; and almost all of them would have cross-bred with the brumbies. When the feed position improved, Hain mustered most of them, but 40, all carrying his 'W7' brand, were left behind. Single-handed, Herbie Hain must have done as much as any man to put new life into the straight-shouldered, ribbed-up animals that were typical brumbies.

The horses live in small mobs, each controlled by a stallion and with territorial rights over an area that can cover many square kilometres. In the high country, this territory usually includes rugged mountain terrain to which they can escape

at any sign of danger. Flight is always the horse's first line of defence.

A mob is no larger than the stallion can control on his own, for he never shares his mares. They are fickle creatures, likely to go off with any other stallion who turns up, if their own leader has his back turned. Twelve is a common size for a mob, 15 is large and 20 rare.

The rest of the mob are fillies and colts. Colts, however, are only allowed to remain with the mob whilst they pose no threat to the stallion's supremacy. As soon as a colt reaches an age when he could compete, he is driven away. Sometimes four or five colts are found running together and these have usually been evicted from the same mob by a stallion rightly distrustful of their intentions towards his mares.

Normally the stallion runs at the back of the herd, keeping his mares moving and in order, ensuring that there are no stragglers. Only when danger looms does he move to the front, taking the lead and guiding the mob to safety.

Horses are among the most successful of all surviving species. For hundreds of thousands of years they survived, despite the attacks of flesh-eating predators, relying on their two great attributes, their legs for running and their eyes for warning, coupled with an extraordinary instinct for sensing danger.

They cope well with almost any weather, but like man, they can be caught unaware by sudden winter storms. The names of creeks and hills bear witness to their occasional fallibility. Mount Ethridge, close to Kosciusko, was long known as Dead Horse Mountain after seventeen brumbies were found dead there when the snows of a particularly heavy winter melted; and nearby Dead Horse Gap acquired its name in the same way.

Paterson wrote a poem which he called simply "Brumby's Run", after a Sydney Supreme Court judge had asked what a brumby was. Part of it goes as follows:

On odds and ends of mountain land,
On tracks of range and rock,
Where no one else can make a stand,
Old Brumby rears his stock.

A wild, unhandled lot they are
Of every shape and breed,

They venture out 'neath moon and star
Along the flats to feed.

But when the dawn makes pink the sky,
And steals along the plain,
The brumby horses turn and fly
Towards the hills again.

Self-protection has made them essentially nocturnal animals, the main reason why they are so seldom seen. Weakened in physique they may be now, but they have lost none of their cunning.

Most of the old timers refuse to accept that the brumbies do any serious damage to the ecology. Indeed, they argue that the horses keep the bush down to a manageable level, protecting it against fire, keeping open tracks that would otherwise quickly become overgrown and making accessible otherwise impenetrable country.

Ecologists and park managers, of course, see it quite differently. They point to the damage to the soil and the bogs that a single mob can cause as it passes or stops to drink and graze. They claim that there is no room for a large animal like a horse, particularly one that moves around in herds, in country as fragile as the high country and in which they are totally alien. They argue that the horses should be treated as vermin and controlled by culling. The result is almost never a fair contest. They are poisoned, trapped and shot from hovering helicopters with high-powered rifles fitted with telescopic sights. It is hard not to give all one's sympathy to the horses.

Men have always found a use for the wild horses in the high country. They are a cash crop when they are rounded up and sold, and they have been packhorse and saddle horse and even food. An old gold-prospecting hermit, Charlie Carter, who lived at Tin Mines, survived for years on the horses. His staple diet was foal. Others have used mobs of horses to break open tracks in the snow each winter, to allow their cattle to reach safety when the snow is too deep for them to break out alone. And, of course, as the quarry in brumby running, they have given many mountain people their sport and their thrills.

Brumby running was always above all a sport and an exceedingly dangerous one that had no place for the weak-hearted and the novice. They called it wild horse hunting in the high country for many years, and somehow that is more descriptive of the risks of running horses over country where 'The hidden ground was full of wombat holes, and any slip was death'. In the tangle of timber and undergrowth, where every step can spell disaster and where the mountainsides drop almost vertically into deep ravines, it requires skill and courage in high measure, not only from the rider, but from his horse.

Some of the best runs were when a good horse got away. The most the horse's owner was likely to see of it was a glimpse of it flying by with its new mob. If he was lucky it was brought in with a mob that had been trapped and was recognised before it was sold.

If a horse was really valuable, its owner might put up a generous reward and the brumby runners would come from every direction to share in the chase. That was how Banjo Paterson began the story of *The Man from Snowy River*:

There was movement at the station, for the word had
  passed around
That the colt from old Regret had got away,
And had joined the wild bush horses—he was worth a
  thousand pound,
So all the cracks had gathered to the fray.
All the tried and noted riders from the stations near and
  far
Had mustered at the homestead overnight,
For the bushmen love hard riding where the wild bush
  horses are,
And the stockhorse snuffs the battle with delight.

17

The discovery of the Monaro

On Thursday 22 May 1823, a naval officer named Captain Mark Currie set out from Bong Bong, a property near Moss Vale, with a small party to explore the unknown country south of Lake George. Fifteen days later, on 6 June, Currie wrote in his diary that they had crossed the "Morrumbidgee" River (it was in fact the Bredbo River, a tributary of the Murrumbidgee), and that riding on to the south, they had observed "down country to a very considerable extent, say 40 miles to the southward of our encampment, bounded on the west by the snowy range of mountains, and on the east by what may probably turn out to be the coast range of mountains".

The existence of snow-capped mountains had been known for years: what Currie discovered was a great expanse of rolling hills and downs to the east of them, whose rich grassland should make them ideal for raising sheep. He noticed too that much of it was strangely treeless.

They met a group of Aboriginals who were terrified of their horses, but from whom they learned that this country, stretching into the far distance, was called Monaroo, their word for a woman's breasts, an apt name for the smooth, rounded hills.

Because his provisions were running low, Currie was forced to turn back, but news of his discovery spread fast. Within a very short time, the first white settlers were heading towards this new country where the peculiar lack of trees meant that they could put their stock to graze immediately without first having to clear it.

Like the Snowy Mountains, the Monaro has vague boundaries. Roughly a trapezoid in shape, it is the area bounded by Jindabyne, Adaminaby, Michelago and Nimmitabel, then extended south from Jindabyne and Nimmitabel to the Victorian border. It is country that varies from mountains and steep gorges, through the hills that gave it its Aboriginal name, to the treeless "plains" that are not really plains at all but the local term used for the bottoms of the broad, eroded valleys and the tablelands.

The treelessness in these valleys is an entirely natural phenomenon which botanists believe is caused by a combination of heavy basalt soil, low rainfall, low temperature and what they term "cold air drainage". Pools of cold air at the bottom of the valleys prevent seedlings from germinating, and because the plains are not high enough to have alpine vegetation, they remain treeless. Further up, on the lighter ridges and steeper slopes that border the valleys, there is woodland, mainly of stunted, gnarled eucalypts, but this ends abruptly at a critical contour.

The plains were evidently inhospitable places for the Aboriginals, providing them with neither shelter, firewood, nor much food. There is almost no evidence of any Aboriginal occupation

(opposite) *Mist hangs over the treeless basalt plains of the Monaro. The treelessness is an entirely natural phenomenon—only some hardy European trees, such as these 100-year old English elms* (above), *grow with any success in the heavy basalt soil.*

there, apart from one or two sites which appear to have been used for quarrying stone. But there is abundant evidence of early occupation elsewhere on the Monaro and the little archaeological work that has been carried out suggests that man first arrived there about 15,000 years ago, or in other words, well before the end of the last ice age.

Two separate groups were flourishing on the Monaro when the Europeans arrived, the Ngarigo and the Wolgai. The Ngarigo occupied the Snowy River valley, upstream from where Delegate is today, then north through the Murrumbidgee valley almost as far as Canberra; the Wolgai were in the upper Murrumbidgee and the Eucumbene above Adaminaby, and had all the country around Kiandra, much of what is now the Australian Capital Territory, and everything in between across to the Murray.

The Aboriginals whom the Europeans encountered were not hostile, and there is no evidence that the Europeans were particularly violent towards them, at least to the extent that they did not trap them or systematically kill them as they did in so many other parts of Australia. It was the Europeans' diseases that took a terrible toll, particularly influenza and syphilis; and inevitably, the very fact of the European occupation meant that the Aboriginals were forced away from their traditional lands and lost many of their vital sources of food.

From every account, both groups were independent, sociable, high-spirited people when they first encountered Europeans. Yet in the briefest of moments, when measured against the time they had lived on the Monaro, they were reduced to pockets of struggling, diseased, degraded individuals, eking out their last miserable years. If one counts a generation as 25 years—and an Aboriginal generation was probably much shorter—there had been about 600 generations of black Australians living on the Monaro before the white settlers arrived and effectively wiped them out in less than three.

The last leader of the Wolgai, the "King of the Monaroo", Murray Jack, as the Europeans dubbed him—and hung a plaque round his neck to inform people—died in 1891; and the last member of the Ngarigo, Biggenhook, died in Cooma in June 1914. He was deaf and dumb.

The first settlers on the Moneroo, or Monaro, were a mixed bunch. (The word was spelt in many ways before Monaro

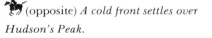 (opposite) *A cold front settles over Hudson's Peak.*

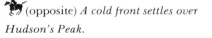 (above) *The history of European settlement on the Monaro stems back to 1823 and relics of these earlier times still abound.*

They all arrived on the Monaro and, with no title to any land, simply squatted on it. The word squatter would go through many shades of meaning over the years, to include those who held their land by licence, the freeholders, and eventually, from this, any wealthy grazier; but it was never more appropriate than in these earliest days of settlement when squatters really were squatters.

They gradually spread out until they reached unoccupied land that suited them and there they halted, turned loose their stock and put up a rough hut to protect them from the elements. The Murrumbidgee, already a broad river by the time it reaches Cooma, with 1500 kilometres still to flow, drew many settlers to its banks, and so did the Snowy River which influences much of the southern half of the Monaro.

Once down near Bombala and Delegate, they moved on to what is now the Victorian border and then across the hills to Suggan Buggan and up on to the Victorian high plains.

The experienced settlers moved very fast to secure the best country and add outstations to their existing runs. The Campbells, for example, who in 1825 had a fine sheep run at Limestone Plains (or Duntroon as it became), had already established an outstation as far south as Delegate by 1827 and were running 22,000 sheep there.

Although Currie is credited with being the first white man to discover the Monaro, it is certain that there were already Europeans further to the west along the Snowy River. The Pendergasts, the oldest of all the high country families, and descendants of an Irish convict, were almost certainly running 400 head of cattle there by 1821. They like to tell how Strzelecki came to the Snowy Mountains, looking for the highest peak to climb, so that he could be the first European to reach the summit of Australia. He saw smoke rising from what he took to be an Aboriginal camp. When he rode over to investigate, however, he found not Aboriginals, but two Pendergast brothers (the sons of John, the convict), who obligingly pointed out the highest mountain, the one that was always last to lose its snow, which they already knew well.

If the records from these early years on the Monaro are sometimes hazy, it is little wonder. Many of the settlers were people who would not have been inclined, or able, to keep

became the accepted spelling in about the 1860s.) There were settlers who were already well established but needed more land, and others, attracted by this rich, free country, who were putting down their first roots. There were emancipists and ticket-of-leave convicts, some wanting to make a new start, and some, as an observer wrote, whose only interest was to carry on "an extensive system of depredation upon the flocks, herds and property of the established settlers".

(opposite) *The harsh and changeable seasons of the Monaro.*

Many of the old cemeteries of the Monaro are a who's who of early pioneering families. Christ Church (above left) and the Pendergast graves at Cottage Creek (left). (below) This ruin on the Monaro Highway was once part of the area's early settlement.

a diary. The striking thing is how many of the problems and obstacles that the graziers face today would have been immediately recognised by their predecessors 150 years before. The harsh, unpredictable Monaro weather is no kinder; drought, disease, greedy lenders and unsympathetic governments all come in their due season to plague them. They are still undervalued and misunderstood by a nation which has no idea how much it needs them, or how desperate the farmer's plight can be. Then, as now, they were vulnerable to many forces outside their control. Both shared expectations of plenty and both experienced the harsh reality that, all too often on the Monaro, plenty turns out to be only a mirage.

Squatters, settlers and peacocks

In 1828, the colony of New South Wales had a tiny population of fewer than 37,000 Europeans, most of them convicts and emancipists. About 1.2 million hectares of land had been alienated, given away or sold by the Crown, yet less than a tenth of this had been cleared and less than a 40th was under cultivation.

For the government, hopelessly strapped for cash and struggling to keep some control on development, the enormous areas of virgin land that were being opened up by exploration were a mixed blessing and in 1829 the governor decreed that settlement would only be allowed in what became known as the Nineteen Counties.

The Nineteen Counties consisted of about nine million hectares within which roads would be built, a police force provided to maintain law and order, and a local system of justice introduced. Settlement outside the Nineteen Counties was prohibited altogether, under threat of prosecution; and the whole of the Monaro, as well as the mountain country, lay outside the proclaimed areas, which ended just south of Michelago.

Predictably, the controls were received with unrelieved fury by the settlers at the southern end of the colony. They viewed the new laws as bureaucratic interference and ignored both them and the land commissioners who were appointed to administer them. Those who were already on the Monaro stayed put; those who were planning to move there still did, and took their stock with them.

By 1834, the laws were so ineffectual that the surveyor-general, Thomas Mitchell, after an extensive tour of the Nineteen Counties and the unsettled lands, reported to the governor that there was now as much stock outside the permitted areas as within them. Finally, in 1836, the government relented. The squatters were for the first time given grazing rights, and for a fee of about ten pounds a year, based on the carrying capacity of the run, they received a licence.

All Crown land in the colony outside the Nineteen Counties was divided into nine districts, each with a commissioner to administer the licensing laws and to mediate in boundary disputes and in any conflicts with the Aboriginals.

Commissioner John Lambie, a surveyor, set up his office in Cooma, which was still little more than a sheep run, and so ensured that it would become the most important town on the Monaro. His enormous squattage district stretched from Michelago to Orbost at the mouth of the Snowy River, from the peaks of the Snowy Mountains east to the Pacific.

Although they were now on their runs legally and for a peppercorn rent, the squatters were

Although many of the earliest buildings were built from wooden slabs, the treelessness of the Monaro forced most settlers to build with the plentiful basalt stone of the area. These stone structures have more readily survived the rigours of the harsh Monaro climate.

25

still far from satisfied, for the one thing they wanted above all, security of tenure, was still denied them. Their licences were only valid for 12 months and were held entirely at the whim of the government which could withdraw them at any time, or sell them over the heads of the squatters at auction. If this happened, they did not even receive compensation for the improvements they had made.

In consequence, during this early period, the squatters on the Monaro ensured that almost no improvements were made. Runs remained unfenced and buildings were as basic as they could make them, usually of bark or slab. Even digging dams to water stock was avoided wherever possible, yet this was a time when wool was vital for the colony's economy and when the settlers on the Monaro sheep runs needed every incentive to make them as efficient as possible. It was a formula for conflict and the Monaro graziers have never shirked a fight.

They were now putting forward a well-organised and very vocal lobby and Sir George Gipps, the governor since 1838, had few more difficult or persistent problems on his hands than their claims. He was prepared to make some concessions, but not nearly as many as they were demanding. Nor was tenure the only issue on which he found himself at loggerheads with them. He ended the assignment of convict labour to these settlers, for example, shortly before transportation to New South Wales ended in 1840, and then refused to give them the coolie labour they wanted in its place.

Gipps, surely the most maligned of all the colony's early governors, finally left for England in 1846 exhausted and disillusioned. The *Sydney Morning Herald* farewelled him ungraciously as "the worst Governor New South Wales has ever had". The truth, as history would show, was far different, for he was one of the most devoted and able of all the colonial governors.

Within nine months of his departure, new orders, which unknown to his critics, Gipps had been instrumental in drafting, came into effect. Monaro squatters were granted 14-year leases with generous pre-emptive rights. They could purchase up to 640 acres (260 hectares) of any part of their leases, and if their runs were sold over their heads at the end of the 14 years, they would now receive compensation for any improvements they had made.

If 640 acres was only a fraction of what were sometimes enormous leases, it was enough for a wily landholder to secure permanent tenure over his whole run. By using a practice known as "peacocking", which involved buying up river frontages and other choice parts of the lease, a squatter could leave the rest of the lease without access to water, making it useless to anyone else.

They supplemented peacocking with the extensive use of dummies, or front men, who held parcels of land for them, including any other prime land they needed but could not own because of the 640-acre limit.

Whatever Gipps had in mind, the effect of his legislation was that the squatters were now almost immovably entrenched. It was a resounding victory, but anything less would have made no sense: in some years, a stocking rate of more than two sheep to the acre was excessive. Scale of operation has always been the key to prosperity on the Monaro and fragmentation has spelt disaster.

The immediate consequence of the squatters' new security was that they began to make long overdue improvements and particularly to build more permanent and elaborate homes. It was no coincidence that women now began to arrive on the Monaro.

In the early years of settlement, there had been almost no women there and when the explorer John Lhotsky made a journey through the region in 1834, he did not see a single white woman south of Michelago. For as long as the settlers refused to make improvements, conditions were so primitive that no woman would have wanted to live there for long: and even those squatters who came from established and wealthy families and who were trying to live as normal a life as they could in these very abnormal conditions, rarely had women with them.

A typical squatter's hut was built from stringy-bark or ironbark, whose stems needed no additional straightening; and the native pine, *Callitris*, was used for the same purpose when it was available. The bark of the stringy-bark and the ironbark in particular separated easily and came away in long sheets so that it made an ideal building material, as the Aboriginals had known for thousands of years. The bark was nailed to the uprights and formed the walls as well as the roof, and the entire hut took a skilled bushman only a few hours to put together.

Huts were also built of slabs, or thick planks, with the wall that contained the chimney made of stone. There were usually two rooms, the larger one doubling as living room and main bedroom, and containing the fireplace where all the cooking was done; the second was another bedroom that served as well as a store-room. Over the whole hut there was usually a loft.

Cooking was done over the open fire. Chains of various lengths were hung from a crossbar in the chimney. On the end of each chain was a hook, and the cook (everyone was a cook) selected the chain that was the right length, depending on whether he wanted to cook fast or slowly. A skilled cook could regulate the billy or the oven as accurately as any modern stove, and by varying the types of wood that he used, he could control the temperature of

🐎 *Remnants of the early pioneering days—a well preserved slab building at Micalago Station and a dray at Numeralla (opposite).*

🐎 (above) *Man and his dog—an invincible working team. For men such as Jim Parkes, born at the turn of the century, the working dog has remained an indispensable workmate.*

(opposite) *Many of the early grazing properties utilised their mountain leases to spell their lower country during the summer months.*
(above left) *Herb Mawson built Mawson's Hut on the Bobundara lease in the Jagungal–Snowy Plains area.*

Remnants of the stock and dog proof fence which enclosed Mawson's 10,000 sheep are still to be seen in the area.

the fire itself. Native pine, for example, burns at a very high temperature and still has a place beside the solid fuel ovens of many women in the high country, to be used when they are baking and need a hot fire.

Toilet facilities were either non-existent or very primitive, and when they did exist, they were usually little more than a trench dug a short distance from the house. The insanitary conditions and disease were never far apart.

There was no entertainment, of course, unless the men, and later their families, made it for themselves. A picture show man, with "Alpine Pictures" painted on the side of his truck, travelled around the Monaro communities, and occasionally a wandering theatre company passed through, but that wasn't until years later.

John Lhotsky described a typical Sunday on the Monaro as he saw it. "It is usual among the men of Menero [another spelling] to pass their Sundays in mutual calls, having shaved and cleaned themselves," he wrote in his diary. "However, all look extremely masculine, and the conversation also is mostly confined to the topic, 'In such-and-such a hut, they have grog.' "

The arrival of women had a profound social effect. Some quite elaborate homes were built, to soften, one imagines, the blow of what must often have been a stunning culture shock. These homesteads were not as grand as some of those which sprang up around the turn of the century, designed by fashionable architects of the time such as George Cochrane, but they must have seemed like palaces compared with the squatters' huts that they replaced.

A visitor to the Monaro in 1872 wrote, "The homesteads of Monaro are in general very comfortable, neat and substantial and some of them replete with the conveniences and adornments of the most refined life." Nor was this surprising, for some of the squatters came from very well-to-do families. They brought their possessions with them and could afford to surround themselves with servants to ease the lives of their wives.

From their first days there, women played a vital role in the life of the Monaro. Today, there are many sheep runs which would not survive at all were it not for the financial contribution that the graziers' wives make, yet without abandoning any of their other roles. A century ago, they may not by necessity have been teachers or writers,

Many early homesteads incorporated a separate kitchen block, joined to the dining room by a covered walkway, although very few houses of this design survive today (above). *The women who followed the early settlers to the Monaro made these homes more civilised, and established gardens to soften and protect the buildings. Many of these have developed into magnificent gardens, such as those at Micalago Station* (above right) *and Yandra* (right).

or have driven school buses to supplement the farm income, but the practical contribution they made was no less important.

Most of the more elaborate homesteads from this time had little planned formality. Typically, they were long, single-storeyed buildings with many of the rooms opening on to a wide verandah which kept the house warm in winter and cool in summer. Nearly all of them had a separate kitchen block, reached by a covered walkway, which was quite often the original squatter's hut. Around the house, a cool, shady garden was laid out, often very English in design.

The home was also a self-contained working unit, so not far from the house would be the squatter's office, a cottage for extra guests and store-rooms; and further out still, the rooms for the farm hands and shearers.

Not many of these homes have survived, because one of the more unfortunate traditions has been that as successive, ever grander houses were built on the big runs, those which they replaced were abandoned. Very occasionally one finds three or even four homesteads on the larger properties, from the original slab cottage where it all began, each a mark of the improving fortunes of the squatting family.

One would expect these sometimes elegant and often very large houses, with their formal gardens, English names and faint echoes of genteel tea parties, to look quite incongruous out on the Monaro plains. In fact, the tradition of building spacious homes with wide eaves and verandahs, soft contrasts of shade and sunlight and a silhouette that hugged the ground, lets them blend harmoniously into the landscape.

Micalago Station, situated at the northern edge of the Monaro plains, has remained in the Ryrie family for five generations. This unique collection of buildings reflects the history of the Monaro, with earliest simple slab structures still remaining. A gracious colonial homestead, incorporating later additions by Professor Wilkinson, encloses the beautifully planted courtyards and overlooks the charming garden.

Early life on the Monaro

The first sheep on the Monaro probably belonged to Dr David Reid who had a run at Reid's Flat, where Bunyan is today, just north of Cooma. He brought breeding sheep from Camden Park, not long after Currie had returned to Bong Bong to announce his discovery of rich new grasslands to the south.

It was not until the 1870s that there was any purposeful improvement of the Monaro flocks, by culling and selective breeding. For a long time, the only sheep on the Monaro were unprepossessing looking creatures—"bastards every one, with small frames and impaired constitutions", a visitor wrote in the 1870s. They were highly prone to disease and though the blowfly was not the scourge that it became for the highly refined merino, with its folded, wrinkled skin into which the flies can burrow, there was no shortage of other calamities waiting to strike.

Two of the most prevalent were catarrh, a highly contagious pulmonary infection which could kill off a flock of 10,000 sheep inside a week, and scab. Though not a killer, scab could be even more disastrous financially: like catarrh, it could spread like wildfire through a flock and not even the wool was spared. The whole animal was worthless.

It was William Bradley, one of the most important pioneers on the Monaro, who was the first to introduce a measure of control of both diseases. Using his experience on his father's tobacco farm, which he had taken over and expanded, he produced a nicotine solution which he brewed up by mixing tobacco leaves with water. By instituting a strict regime of washing, shearing and then daubing the affected parts of the sheep with this concoction, he was able to eradicate scab throughout his flocks.

There was still no treatment for catarrh, but what Bradley did establish was that by destroying any sheep the moment the first symptoms appeared, and then boiling them down for tallow, he was able to save the rest of the flock.

The boiling pots became a well-used feature of many of the larger runs, while mobile pots travelled around the country serving smaller settlers who did not have their own facilities. At times the price of stock was so low that both sheep and cattle were worth more for tallow than for their meat. Tallow was in great demand for candles and soap and by the 1850s it was already a million pound a year export industry. During times of depression, in the middle of the nineteenth century, a sheep might fetch only sixpence for its meat: boiled down for tallow, which was fetching twenty-eight pounds a ton in London, the squatters could get at least seven shillings for it.

The first sheep were brought to the Monaro in the 1830s and have become the backbone of the area's grazing industry. Don McNee of Caringo, Cooma, a descendant of early settlers the Kiss and O'Mara families, still works the land selected by his ancestors.

Banjo Paterson's High Country

🐎 *A reminder of the last century, this shepherd's fold and drop timber yard were vital in an era before the advent of wire fencing.*

The sheep was skinned, thrown into a huge vat and boiled. The smell was disgusting and carried for miles, and the squatters hated to see their capital assets being boiled down for candles; but tallow saved many of them. In one year, Brodribb, Bradley's senior manager, sent 1700 cattle and several thousand sheep to be boiled down, and in a move that would have brought him unpleasant headlines a century later, he destroyed 1200 calves to allow their mothers to get fat, so they would be more profitable in the boiling pot.

There are still a few of the old pots around the Monaro and a few names of creeks and hills are timeless reminders. Leatherbarrel Creek, which rises under North Ramshead near the source of the Snowy River, got its name from the barrels used to carry the tallow out. They were made from a bullock hide with the corners cut off and then folded and sewn together, leaving an opening at one end. When it was full, the cask weighed more than 100 kilograms.

For the first 50 years of settlement, squatters relied heavily on shepherds to watch over their flocks and to protect the sheep from the constant danger of being pulled down and killed by dingoes. If their own homes were sometimes modest and their work harsh, those of most of these shepherds were unrelievedly wretched.

They were often alone in the bush for months on end, enduring every kind of weather from drought and torrential rain to blizzard and searing heat. The job was so lonely and the conditions so bad that the shepherds became known as hatters because so many of them became as mad as hatters, and the suicide rate among them was notorious.

They existed in such squalour that they were permanently filthy and diseased. A few built themselves semi-permanent huts, but many, constantly on the move, either carried around with them a skimpy dog kennel-type of hut, or used brushwood to make a rough shelter that gave them little protection against the wind and the rain. At worst, they lived among the rocks, laying lengths of brushwood to form a roof. They had a trick for ridding their huts of the fleas which were constantly on their bodies and in their clothes: they drove a dozen sheep into their huts. The theory was that the fleas would jump on to the wool and go out with the sheep.

Of course there were exceptions, men who took the job for the money, worked hard, stayed sane and went on to become settlers in their own right. But the enduring picture of the shepherd that has come down to us is of the lonely, half-mad hermit, living in appalling conditions, and alone save only for his dogs and the sheep. "Some are honest and clean," a squatter wrote, describing the shepherds on the Monaro, "but the rest . . . well, they are horrible!"

John Lhotsky on his travels met a convict shepherd, filthy, bare-foot, ragged and suffering from the advanced stages of syphilis, for which there was no one to treat him. Lhotsky wrote that it reminded him forcefully that he was "in a land of banishment and expiation".

The shepherds' duties were unrelievedly monotonous except at lambing time. Even many years later, when fencing had largely made the shepherds redundant and their conditions had immeasurably improved, their duties had hardly varied since biblical times. They minded their flocks by day and at dusk drove them into hurdles made from rough timber and scrub, or stone. On the larger runs, they often worked as a team, two tending the flocks by day and the third, a watchman, overseeing them at night. It was the watchman's task to count the sheep in each evening and keep them safe in the darkness when they were most vulnerable to attack by dogs.

By the mid-nineteenth century shepherds were paid about 20 pounds a year, and a good employer would supplement this with flour, sugar and tea and allow them to kill sheep for their rations. For many years, they were bound by the Masters and Servants Act which gave the master almost everything and the servant practically nothing—even to complain could be interpreted as neglect of duty, punishable by imprisonment.

With conditions like this, it was difficult to find anyone who would take on the job. Any free settler worth his salt wanted to have his own flock, and the failed squatters, many of whom turned to drink to drown their woes, were considered to be highly unreliable. Often the only men who were available and willing to take on the work were discharged or ticket-of-leave convicts, men on the run from the police and those who were unemployable in any other job. At times, would-be employers were reduced to waiting outside the police courts to pay the fines of offenders to keep them out of gaol, in return for time spent working as a shepherd.

Shearing has changed little over the years. Although blade shearing has given way to mechanisation, basic skills remain important.

(left) *A Monaro sheep sale.*

In fact recently released convicts often adapted well to the work. Conditions in prison were still so appalling that they were hardened to anything and at least as shepherds they had plenty of food and freedom. Many convicts used it as a means of rehabilitating themselves.

When transportation to New South Wales ended in 1840, it became even more difficult to get shepherds. Where it was normally considered that a flock of 500 sheep was the most that a man could handle properly on his own, on some stations this number doubled and then doubled again, and inevitably the condition of the sheep suffered.

It was the arrival of fencing which signalled the beginning of the end for shepherds. Fencing on any scale was not introduced into Australia until the 1860s, and barbed wire not for another ten years after that; and the Monaro and the high country were even slower to take advantage of them. The runs were so large and the terrain often so difficult to fence, that the squatters found it much cheaper to rely on shepherds for as long as possible.

After the gold rush at Kiandra ended in 1861, there were many Chinese around who provided a cheap source of labour. They were used on the Monaro to build walls and folds from the basalt rock that lay everywhere. Stooping low from dawn to dusk, collecting the stones and building the walls, it was back-breaking work for which they were paid eight shillings a chain, which was about 20 metres.

For the settlers who had to meet the requirement of making improvements to their selections of at least a pound an acre before they could obtain the freehold, these Chinese-built stone walls were a double investment. They can still be seen around the Monaro, but many were pulled down during the rabbit plague because they became perfect harbours for the rabbits.

Fencing meant that the old breed of shepherd at last began to die out, but there was a price to pay. For all their shortcomings, most of the shepherds took good care of their sheep and achieved very high lambing figures. When they went, and the ewes and the lambs were left to fend for themselves, there was a striking fall in the lambing rate. But in almost every other regard, the end of the era of the shepherds was lamented by no one and least of all, by most of the shepherds themselves.

Communications in the high country had improved

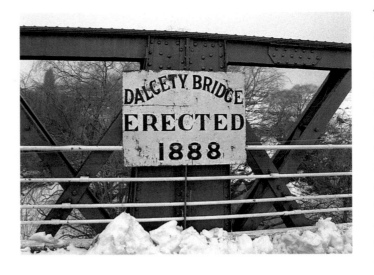

Childhood deaths, as the old graveyards throughout the Monaro poignantly testify, were all too common. Many of the large pastoral stations had their own graveyards which tell of epidemics and sickness, such as this one where seven month-old Clarence Australia Kiss was buried, six weeks after his mother, Martha Kiss (opposite).

The century-old Dalgety Bridge is one of the Monaro's earliest, built after a flood washed the punt away.

(centre) Merino studmaster John Shiels copes with one of the many realities of a Monaro winter. Monaro stock are amongst the most sought-after in the country for their ability to survive and thrive in the harshest of climates (below).

Angus cattle are bred throughout the Monaro and the area has come to be regarded as the state's major black cattle breeding region. Angus breeder Bill Herbert moves a mob of cows with his grand-daughter, Virginia.

dramatically after the discovery of gold at Kiandra. Bullock tracks and packhorse trails were opened up all through the mountains and across the Monaro. By the end of 1860, there was a road linking Cooma and Kiandra where 12 months before there had been no road within 12 kilometres of the place.

Cooma saw its first motor car in 1901, although it was not until several years after this that anyone in the district actually owned one (it was sent back in its box because no one could start it!). Well into the century, bullock trains were still a common sight on the roads, often with 16 bullocks pulling them. In 1910, a train passed through Cooma, pulled by 76 bullocks, dragging a 26 ton boiler to the Kyloe copper mine.

Although the roads improved, they were still often blocked

by the rivers and creeks before bridges were built. Particularly during the snow-melt, they could rise by metres overnight and turn the safest crossings into dangerous torrents that could sweep away a man and a horse. Frequently large areas of the Monaro were cut off and some of the busiest stock crossings were among the most dangerous places.

Jindabyne, for example, was notorious for the number of people who were drowned in the Snowy River there, as they did at Dalgety, a short distance downstream. Many of the settlers could not swim properly, especially those who had come from Britain (not until the second half of the nineteenth century was the medieval prejudice overcome in Europe that outdoor bathing helped to spread the great epidemics that periodically swept across Europe, and so was to be actively discouraged).

Punts were established at many of the Monaro crossings but even these could be lost when the rivers rose. The punt at Dalgety disappeared altogether one night in 1870 in a huge flood, and in 1852, the entire village at Mill Angle, or present day Tumut, was washed away with heavy loss of life.

On the Murrumbidgee and several other rivers, flying foxes were used to cross the swollen water, and right up until the construction of the hydro-electric scheme, when its level was largely controlled by the Tantangara dam, the Murrumbidgee in spate could be a very dangerous river. Ironically, some of the worst flooding on record occurred in the years of severest drought.

Drought on the Monaro is so common and can last for so long that it is probably the norm, not the exception, in spite of the graziers' eternal optimism. When the rains fail, the tablelands turn into a parched and bare dust-bowl, as lifeless as anything on the continent. In conditions like this one would expect to find only a few scraggy sheep with hardly enough energy to survive, yet miraculously, this is not what happens. Losses amongst lambs can be depressingly high, but even on the most terrible rock-strewn country, there is pick, supplemented by hand-feeding, that keeps the sheep in excellent condition. The rich basalt soil ensures that what little grass does emerge is rich in supplements.

The second miracle of the Monaro is that within so short a time of a drought that seemed interminable while it lasted, the whole landscape can be transformed by good rain into rolling green hills as lush as any English countryside.

The grazier today faces a life that is as demanding and uncompromising as any his forebears may have confronted. His destiny still lies for a great part in forces quite outside his control; in the lap of the gods, the politicians and the bureaucrats, who may never in their lives have seen a sheep run, but who determine where and for how much the graziers' produce may be sold.

Not many of the largest early runs have survived intact. Often properties were broken up among the children of the first settlers, then divided and divided again down the generations. But the grazier can now produce carcass weights five times those of the bastard sheep of a century and a half ago, with their small frames and impaired constitutions,

and wool weights ten times greater. It is as true today, however, as it was 150 years ago that the farmer, as John F. Kennedy put it, "is the only man in our economy who buys everything at retail, sells everything he sells at wholesale—and pays the freight both ways".

For those who love the Monaro it has a most powerful appeal, soft and inviting one moment, lonely, cruel and desolate the next. But never monotonous, and never quite like any other part of Australia.

Horses are still used for mustering in this stony basalt country. Although motorbikes have superseded the horse in many areas, the rocky nature of the Monaro has meant that the sure-footed horse continues to play an important role in the management of many properties.

The early graziers

Drawn by the security of the new licences, some remarkable men arrived on the Monaro. Benjamin Boyd, that extraordinary entrepreneur, took advantage of one of the periodic slumps in the grazing industry in the mid-1840s and within two years accumulated fourteen runs on the Monaro, totalling more than 100,000 hectares—all for 40 pounds a year! Disastrously, he used "blackbirded" labour from the Pacific islands.

More lasting was William Bradley, who eventually owned runs that stretched in a closely linked chain for 80 kilometres from Cooma to Bombala. By 1864, he had 20 runs and more than 120,000 hectares.

The son of a former army sergeant who had been granted land near Goulburn after being the first settler to grow tobacco successfully in the colony, Bradley managed his land well. A huge man physically, he could shear a sheep and drive a bullock train as well as any of his hands, and when faced with a labour shortage in the 1840s, instead of cutting wages or turning to the blackbirders as Boyd had done, he paid his men slightly more than the other landowners and was rewarded with a full and loyal workforce.

He showed the same shrewdness in his selection of the managers on his many runs. He shared all his knowledge with them and later helped many of them on to selections of their own. The link with Bradley runs like a thread through many of the families that are still prominent on the Monaro. His senior manager, William Brodribb, the son of an attorney who had been transported for administering illegal oaths, became a successful selector in his own right; and another, James Litchfield, went on to found Hazeldean, the Monaro's most influential sheep stud.

Nor was it only his managers who benefited from their association with him. Two of the oldest Monaro families, the Hains and the Agnews, are descended from two of Bradley's shepherds. The first Hain in Australia came out in *Petrel* as a freeman, while the first Agnew was an Irish convict, transported for conspiracy to murder.

A number of the early settlers were Scottish, tough, resilient men who persisted through every crisis and were careful, cautious managers. Robert Campbell was running 20,000 sheep by 1827, and another highlander, William Jardine, made his mark and a fortune. His family still run the country that he pioneered at Nimmitabel.

Not all the successful settlers on the Monaro were expatriate Britons. By the 1830s, the colony had been established for more than 40 years and there was no lack of adventurous currency

(opposite) *The Sutherns from Dalgety are one of the few remaining NSW families to make their annual pilgrimage to high summer grazing country. Attacks from wild dogs who roam onto the plains from the adjoining National Park, however, make their freehold on Snowy Plains increasingly untenable. The Suthern's sheep are seen here returning to lower pastures after a killing rampage in which 23 sheep were lost in one week.*

(above) *The Monaro is one of the country's major Merino breeding districts. These Merino wethers show the characteristics of good constitution and heavy fleeces.*

41

lads, born in Australia, who were independent, resourceful and willing to load their worldly possessions on to a bullock train and head for this unknown country.

It was not at all unusual to find a 14 or 15 year old managing a run single-handed, or with only an illiterate shepherd to help him. The historic property of Gegedzerick, near Berridale, was opened up by 16 year-old teenager Richard Brooks who in 1827 was soon running 5000 sheep and 1000 cattle on a huge run.

For the squatters, some of whom were paying 30 pounds a year for 18,000 hectares of some of the best land in the colony, the Government's land policy was eminently satisfactory. The growing clamour for reform was therefore certainly not coming from them, but from those who bitterly resented the situation that was increasingly seen to be

Angus McPhie, who once held a large lease in the remote Grey Mare–Dicky Cooper area, remains active in the running of his family property at Ravensworth, Cooma.

Angus McPhie and Bill Keevers brand cattle at Ravensworth (right).

preserving the best Crown land for this powerful squattocracy. "A great evil" was typical of the descriptions of the system that the politicians, their ears closely attuned to public opinion, were becoming fond of using. It was clearly only a matter of time before radical changes would have to be made to make some of this land available to more people.

The reality was that on the Monaro, it made no sense to break up the big runs. It is country for grazing, not agriculture, and size has always been critical. The minimum size for a viable sheep run is 2500 acres, or about 1025 hectares, and one of the reasons why so many of the soldier-settlers failed years later, when they tried to run sheep on the land they received from a grateful government, was that they were simply not given enough of it. Very few received more than 1800 acres.

New laws, the Robertson Land Acts, were finally passed in 1861. Ostensibly aimed at putting the "small man" on to the land to expand agricultural production, they allowed "selectors" to settle on a block of Crown land, regardless of whether or not it was already part of someone else's existing lease.

Because of the shortage of surveyors in the colony, free settlement even before survey was allowed. The selectors decided which land appealed to them (initially the block had to be between 40 and 320 acres in area, though this was later increased to 640), paid a deposit of five shillings an acre and then, provided the land had not been selected by someone else, were given immediate possession.

The balance of 15 shillings an acre was supposed to be paid within three years, but even if a selector failed to meet this date, his tenure was still secure as long as he paid interest on the balance at three per cent a year. The only other requirement was that he should live on his selection for three years and improve it to the extent of at least a pound an acre. If he fulfilled these conditions and paid the balance of the purchase price, he received freehold title and could then select another block and with it a grazing licence, or "pre-lease", to land three times the size of the original selection.

Not surprisingly, to the squatter the selector was a serious and most unwelcome threat and it made no difference if he was a genuine farmer, or one of the many unscrupulous land sharks whose main interest lay in blackmailing the squatters into buying them out at an exorbitant rate.

The squatters did have some rights, but not many. They had a pre-emptive right, for example, to one twenty-fifth of their runs and to land on which they had made improvements, such as their homestead, the shearing sheds, dams and fences; and they also had the same rights of selection on their own land as anyone else. Both could be used to great effect to exploit the new laws.

The squatters could, and certainly often did, make life as difficult as they could for the selectors. Access to water was always a crucial issue to both the squatter and the selector. The practice of peacocking gave the squatter a means by which he could limit the water supply to a selector's property. Then, by denying access to their own rivers and waterholes if the selectors' creeks dried up, the squatters were provided with a most effective weapon to use against those who they saw as encroaching upon their land and livelihood.

The Robertson Land Acts' requirement that a selector had to live on the land for three years to qualify for the freehold, could be manipulated by the squatters. By having as many as four portions joining at one point, and then building one house which straddled all four of them, they were quickly able to increase their land holdings. This was done at the lovely old property Coolamine.

With a little ingenuity, the squatters could also get round the compulsory improvements that had to be made. Many genuine improvements certainly were made—clearing, building stone fences, ringbarking trees and erecting sheds and a home; but there were other ways of deceiving the inspectors. By building movable fences and huts, for example, they could place them at various strategic points around the run and then hurriedly have them moved to another site just ahead of the inspector.

The main problem for the small settlers was not how to get land, but how to hold on to it. They rarely had access to the banks, and the pastoral companies were naturally more in sympathy with the established squatters. They knew better than anyone that trying to make a 320 acre sheep run financially viable was an almost impossible task.

Many of the selectors could put down their deposits of five shillings an acre, but when they needed money for

improvements, or to pay off the balance of the purchase price, it was often very hard to find. All too often, the squatters had only to bide their time, do nothing to help the selectors, and their old land would come back on the market where they could snap it up at auction. To their critics they insisted always that they were fighting for their very survival.

It was not only outsiders who took advantage of the new laws. There were many people already on the Monaro who were ideally placed to make good selections. James Litchfield, William Bradley's manager, had often noticed as he rode backwards and forwards between Coolringdon and another of Bradley's properties, Myalla, near Cooma, that the sheep always seemed to gravitate to one particular spot.

With this knowledge, he selected 320 acres which he called Springwell, and built a cottage for himself and his wife. A few years later, he selected another site, not far away, where he built a second home, Hazeldean, and there established the stud that has remained at the forefront of Australia's merino breeding for more than 100 years.

Litchfield built up his holdings by selection and purchase until by the mid-1880s, he owned more than 8000 hectares. He freely admitted to a parliamentary select committee that he had used dummies to build up his holding, justifying it on the grounds that fragmentation would have been disastrous, not only for him personally, but for the colony's entire sheep breeding industry.

In 1883, a Royal Commission reached the same conclusion, that the Robertson Land Acts had been a disaster. More than 29 million acres of Crown land had been alienated to expand agricultural production, yet less than half a million acres were even under cultivation. Legally these Land Acts were equally destructive, for they offered land to the selectors that had already been legally assigned to the squatters. Both could claim equal rights under the law, but inevitably it was the richer, more powerful and tactically far more firmly entrenched squatters who won almost every dispute.

With all its faults, the system dragged on into the 1890s before the first steps were taken to dismantle it. At the time when the Man from Snowy River rode out, the rule of the squatter was still paramount.

Mick Pendergast is a descendant of the earliest mountain pioneers, the Pendergast brothers, who were thought to be in the area before its official discovery in 1823.

Cooma: town of contrasts

There is nearly always an element of luck that determines which embryo communities will develop and prosper and which will remain in sleepy oblivion. Michelago, a village that travellers today bypass without a second glance on their way from Canberra to the snowfields, was a community that for a moment seemed on the point of developing into a thriving township.

It lay on the direct track from Sydney and Goulburn to the new Monaro grazing properties and soon to the Kiandra gold diggings. And once Reid's Flat which today is even more insignificant than Michelago, also had fleeting expectations of riches that came to nothing. Colinton, on the same road, never even got beyond being a name, though it still appears on maps.

Instead, it was a village further south that did not even exist when Michelago and Reid's Flat first began to dream of greater things, that would prosper and expand.

In the 1830s, Kuma was a sheep run. It was well placed to develop into a modest hamlet, for it lay at the point where several roads converged—to the coast, to Bombala and Adaminaby and later to the goldfields. Much more significantly, as it turned out, it was the place where a one-time hawker chose to build a pub and a government public servant called John Lambie to open his office as Commissioner of Lands for the Monaro.

The inn was built by James Kirwan and Lambie held an adjoining 1200 acre paddock. The town's historic Lambie Street ran right up to his front door. With the Crown Lands office and the pub so near each other, it was only a short time before Cooma grew busier and became the focus of affairs for the whole region. By 1856, the population had grown to all of 156, but the population of Sydney was still little more than 50,000.

Just three of the houses were built from brick or stone and the rest were weatherboard or slab. Fire was a constant hazard and Lambie's own house caught fire three times in one year.

It was the discovery of gold at Kiandra in 1859 that was the first major fillip in Cooma's fortunes. Kiandra was only 90 kilometres away and men poured into the town from all parts of the world, as they would do nearly 100 years later to tunnel into the mountains for the hydro-electric scheme.

The banks were among the first to descend on the town when gold was discovered. It took the first bank manager, from the Commercial Banking Company, just over eight days to make the journey from Sydney, but once there was obviously keen to get involved in his new community's life. He organised a cricket match, which he described in a diary. "The wickets were pitched in the unmetalled street [Lambie Street], sides were chosen and my team composed of squatters,

(opposite) *One of Cooma's oldest remaining homes, this stone building is in historic Lambie Street.*

(above) *Frosty morning in Cooma.*

town's major industries, had been turned into an insane asylum within six years of being built as a gaol in 1867.

The hospital was largely financed from fines for drunkenness, and fees for impounded animals. Surgery was carried out there from the start and operations became something of an entertainment. One double amputation was witnessed by "many gentlemen residing in the district, some of whom rode a long distance to be present". The patient on that occasion has good news and bad. He survived the operation, then went mad and had to be carted off to the Liverpool asylum. We are not told why the generous facilities in Cooma were not considered adequate.

Cooma had its own mineral spring, which still bubbles away near the road to Nimmitabel and the coast. It was reputedly beneficial for syphilis, constipation and sore eyes and it also, from every account, tasted foul. A generous measure of rum was the most fancied way of making it palatable and one desperate soul tipped an entire cask of rum into the spring, which retaliated by spewing up bubbling mud for weeks.

Cooma was always a swampy place, prone to the occasional violent flood. Its name came from the Aboriginal word "kuma", or "coombah", meaning a big lake or swamp. The present Centennial Park, a cool, pretty oasis in the middle of the town, was originally a swamp and occasionally a lake.

After the gold rush collapsed, Cooma settled down to nearly 90 years as a prosperous little community servicing one of the finest merino wool producing regions in the world. Its second lease of life came as dramatically as the discovery of gold, when in 1949, it was chosen to be the headquarters of the ambitious new Snowy Mountains Hydro-electric Scheme which tunneled through the mountains and diverted the flow of some of Australia's most magnificent waterways. Within a short time, the town's population swelled from 2000 to 10,000, as people from 50 nations, almost all of them men, poured in.

Work on the scheme went on for two decades, and from being a conservative little country town, Cooma suddenly found that it had become cosmopolitan and sometimes very wild. There were nightclubs and gambling joints, girls came down from the city to relieve the lonely Snowy men of their generous wages, and rivalries brought in from other

A town of contrasts, Cooma nestles among lofty hills, dotted with eucalypts and pines, while European deciduous trees provide magnificent colouring in the chill autumn.

Jews, storekeepers, the police magistrate and a prisoner on bail, scored 97." The game was interrupted by the arrival of the stage coach, bringing the bank's new accountant.

Facilities in the town improved with the new money that came in with the gold rush. The first hospital had been in a series of rented houses and was for treating "paupers, wanderers, severely injured labourers and a few mental cases". By 1858, a proper hospital was being built, as well as an asylum, which appear to have been needed in equal measure. Even the gaunt, granite prison, still one of the

46

countries sometimes erupted into violence.

More than 120 people lost their lives on the construction, far more than had been claimed from the community in two world wars, and you cannot lose 120 people, even if they are strangers, in a small town without something rubbing off. Cooma and the men working in the mountains became a very close community, quite different to any other in Australia.

As the project moved towards completion in the early 1970s, most of the workforce drifted away, but some stayed and Cooma still has a large number of European Australians of many nationalities. The wealth of professional skills that had been brought together to create the hydro-electric scheme was harnessed into a new consultancy company and it was a brave political decision to leave it in a small country town.

Cooma's population has now steadied at about 8000, but more than two and a half million visitors pass through the town each year on their way to the snowfields, or to the mountains in spring and summer. The effect of having a population from so many different nations and backgrounds, occupying themselves in so many different ways—as graziers, servicing the tourists, working as highly skilled professionals for the Snowy Mountains Engineering Corporation, running the prison or servicing everyone else— has created an interesting and and unusual community.

It is remarkable what a century can change. A traveller in 1882 passed through Cooma and found it a busy little community, if not everyone's ideal of a tourist centre. "I cannot say there is much to induce a lengthy stay in Cooma, more especially as in winter time the wind blows very cold and the streets are wholly unformed and the mud is slimy and thick, and the means of entertainment within and without are decidedly thin . . . [The] Chinese question . . . [has] two sides [which] are clearly shown in the little town. There are half a dozen dens at the very entrance, filled full of vice and villainy. Ghoul-like wretches hang about the doors and, within, a din of gambling is heard all night."

But he also remarked on the hills, "lofty on either hand, grand with huge grey rocks", and the pines growing strangely side by side with the eucalypts. And he noticed too the "blue mists at eve and morn that spread a marvellous purple fringe against the paling sky". Cooma always was, above all else, a place of many contrasts.

Gold fever

Time has largely erased the memory of the extraordinary effect that the discovery of gold had on mid-nineteenth century Australia. When the rushes started in 1851, first to Ophir in New South Wales and then to Victoria, men with no knowledge of mining abandoned their jobs and sometimes their families on a whim, and headed for the goldfields beside the seasoned miners, all in search of their fortunes. They went in their thousands, lured by the dream of untold riches.

Doctors, lawyers, shop assistants, clerks, the skilled and unskilled, the old and the young, the lame and the strong, all cast sanity and commonsense to the winds. Seamen deserted their ships, shops were forced to close, law courts no longer functioned and schools closed for lack of teachers. At one time, the entire city of Melbourne was left with five constables.

A few—a very few—found their El Dorado, some gained modest riches; but for the majority, there was nothing, no reward but disillusionment, illness and poverty—and, in spite of all the suffering, for some an insatiable, lifelong addiction to gold mining.

In the first year of production, Victoria's population doubled and it earned one million pounds from its gold. Within three years, its population had increased four-fold as prospectors and fortune-seekers poured into Australia from overseas. Inevitably, though, and quite soon, the surface gold on even the richest fields was exhausted and the miners—or those who could afford it—were forced to turn to deep-shaft mining, which required expensive equipment and considerable capital that few of them possessed. The day of the lone prospector seemed to have passed and there were now thousands of them, unemployed or looking, unwillingly, for work.

Then in November 1859, nine years after Australia had first been gripped by gold fever, the electrifying news reached Melbourne, Sydney and the goldfields, that payable gold had been found high in the Snowy Mountains, and in exactly the kind of country that was best suited to the solitary prospectors relying on luck and the sweat of their own brow. No matter that few of these prospectors had any idea where the Snowy Mountains were until that moment, let alone the conditions they could expect to find when they got there.

Overnight there was a new fever. "Gold," wrote an old miner and bush poet, Jack Barnett, "like war, did stir and fire the blood." Once again a rush was on. Often without even the most rudimentary map, men began to converge on this inaccessible corner of New South Wales.

Tradition has it that two brothers named Pollock made the first discovery of payable gold in the mountains. Every summer they brought their sheep up from the Murray to graze the

It is hard to imagine that 500 people once lived in the secluded valley at Lobbs Hole (left), which was once the main route from Tumut to the goldfields at Kiandra. After the collapse of the goldfields some of the diggers started a copper mine at Lobbs Hole which operated until this century. Today, little remains of this early settlement.

49

The pise ruins of the Washington Hotel at Lobbs Hole on the banks of the Yarrangobilly River are now covered in blackberry bushes and show scant resemblance to the once grand verandah-enclosed building.

hills around Kiandra and spent their time fossicking for gold. Indeed there was hardly a shepherd or cowherd at the time who was *not* looking for gold in the high country and there were at least half a dozen others who claimed to have been first. The government of New South Wales never paid a reward for the discovery (as the Victorian government had done), so there is no official record.

It was common knowledge that there was gold in the hills just waiting to be found. The Reverend William Branwhite Clarke, whose discovery of gold near Bathurst in the early 1840s had been silenced by a nervous Governor Gipps ("Put it away, Mr Clarke," Gipps had told him when he was shown the gold, "or we shall all have our throats cut!") had continued his geological forays into the Snowy

Mountains. In 1852, seven years before the Pollocks' discovery, he had announced that there was gold in the area around Kiandra. He had found it at the junction of the Eucumbene and Snowy Rivers and in several other places along streams and rivers.

The Pollocks made their find in Bullock's Head Creek, the creek that runs close to the road linking Kiandra with Mount Selwyn, and what their fossicking unearthed was not just auriferous rock, but real nuggets. Whether or not they were first, it is beyond dispute that it was their announcement of the find when they returned to Tumbarumba which triggered the rush.

The miners came by any means they could lay their hands on. They came on horseback and on bullock wagons, but mainly they came on foot, carrying their belongings and their mining gear on their backs or pushing them before them in wheelbarrows.

They came over the mountains from Cooma, Goulburn and the Monaro; from Twofold Bay on the coast (it took half the time to make the journey from Sydney to Kiandra if you travelled by sea to Twofold Bay than if you went the whole way overland); and up from the Tumut Valley through dense bush and over steep mountains. For the Victorian miners, a surveyor called Ligar marked out a route by way of the Upper Murray which came into Kiandra through Happy Jacks.

Concerned about missing out on possible revenue, the New South Wales Government stationed additional customs officers on the Victorian border to check smuggling of stores from Victoria.

Jack Barnett wrote a poem, undiscovered until Klaus Hueneke, great modern chronicler of the high country, came upon it and included it in his *Huts of the High Country*. It captured the spirit of a rush which was a long and formidable test of a man's endurance even before he reached the goldfield.

> *From Tumut town they loaded came, like camels in an eastern train.*
> *Their packs so clumsy that they showed them humped and bent beneath the load.*
> *Then up Talbingo from the plain, they raised their strength with thoughts of gain.*
> *For to the fields fresh found they went, with eager hope and fierce intent.*
>
> *Toiling in noonday heat up Bullock Hill, they brewed their tea, then pressed on till*
> *Another camp, another meal, another dawn, would then reveal*
> *Another day, and so they went toward their goal their fever never spent*
> *Until they stood upon that plain Giandarra, which in our way we wrongly call Kiandra.*

And there at Giandarra, wrongly called Kiandra, began an even greater struggle to wrest the gold from the hard, unyielding earth in that harsh, relentless climate.

The harshness of the winters at Kiandra were part of the reason for the mass exodus from the goldfields after only two seasons. Newspaper was as good an insulator as any against the fierce mountain winds.

The few remaining pieces of sluicing equipment and rusted machinery tell little of the years of labour at Kiandra.

A place of ghosts: Kiandra

On 18 January 1860, Assistant Gold Commissioner Robert Lynch wrote to his superior,

"I do myself the honour to report to you the discovery of a new goldfield, situated in Gibson's Plains, or 'Kiandra', about 50 miles north-east of Tumbarumba, with steep mountain ranges and the Tumut River intervening, at the foot of a portion of the Snowy Mountains and about 40 miles south-east of Tumut, but over a mountainous and severe country."

By the time Lynch had despatched his letter, the great rush to Kiandra had already begun. It started in December 1859, barely a month after the Pollock brothers spread the news of their find and by April, there were 15,000 men on the diggings. Yet by March 1861, barely 15 months later, the rush was over and the field was being abandoned as miners in their thousands hurried like lemmings to the end of the next rainbow.

There is little that is tangible to be seen today—the occasional hunk of rusting machinery, the abandoned shafts, an overgrown pile of tailings, a few neglected graves. But when the wind blows over the lonely hills and the mist rolls down into the gloomy canyons, there are ghosts everywhere. This was surely the most human, the most exciting and all too often the most tragic of all the stories that unfolded in the high country.

In its short, hectic life, Kiandra produced some very rich gold, and for some, at least, it lived up to everything it had promised. The then Governor of New South Wales, Sir William Denison, wrote in 1860 to his sister: "The Kiandra gold diggings are to re-establish credit, make money plentiful, relieve the insolvent, find work for the unemployed; but if these should prove to be a delusion, like the Fitzroy diggings in 1859, there will be a fearful smash among the men of business, merchants etc."

There is little tangible evidence of the 15,000 workers once living in Kiandra—a hillside of lupins growing wild, an old iron bedhead and some rusty machinery are all that remain.

Kiandra's gold was no delusion. In 1860 alone, 67,687 ounces (1915 kg) were produced. To put that in perspective, it meant at 1989 prices, this gold would be worth more than 30 million dollars. And this was far short of the true production figure. It included only the gold sold to the Gold Commissioner and sent out with the Gold Escort to Sydney. Many miners preferred to hoard their gold or to send it back to Victoria, and of this production there is no record.

Each miner was entitled to a patch of ground about six metres by six and to another six metres of frontage in the beds of the creeks and rivers. Once the claim was pegged, he had

Within 15 months of the discovery of gold at Kiandra, the goldfields had been virtually deserted, although they did have a brief three year revival from 1900. Yan's store (right), along with the cemetery and stamper battery, are decaying remnants of those hectic years.

just three days to register it and begin work, or the claim was forfeited; and any claim that was not being worked within 48 hours of the boundaries being marked could also be forfeited. Nuggets weighing ten kilograms were found, and over an area of hardly 1.3 square kilometres, the diggings proved as rich as any ever discovered in Victoria or California. The richest finds were in the immediate area around Kiandra township and particularly on New Chum Hill, at the present day turn-off to Mount Selwyn. The hill got its name when three new chums, out from England, naively asked another miner where they should begin digging. The miner shrugged and pointed in the direction of the hill. "Drive a tunnel in that yonder," he told them, to fob them off. Within days they had found gold beyond their wildest dreams.

On 4 June 1860, a contingent of Chinese arrived in Kiandra, the vanguard of what was to be an important influence on the diggings. They had formed themselves into the Celestial Transport Company and carried supplies and provisions in on their backs, including the entire plant for the *Alpine Pioneer and Kiandra Advertiser* which went to print for the first time in August 1860.

There were tens of thousands of Chinese in Victoria, many of them until recently on the goldfields, and most still indebted to a wealthy Chinese master who had paid their fares to Australia in return for an agreed period of labour. These unemployed Chinese had formed enclaves to protect themselves against the growing resentment and hostility of the white Australians. It was here that the seeds of Australia's xenophobia were sown, exploding into the violent and murderous rioting and persecution of the Chinese at Lambing Flat, the rush which followed Kiandra. Kiandra, however, experienced little of this bitterness, perhaps, again fortuitously, because the rush was so short-lived. Although the first batch of about eighty Chinese was soon reinforced by the arrival of hundreds more, the 20,000 who, it was rumoured, were heading for the mountains never materialised.

For the first few months, there was not even a safe in the town and the Gold Commissioner had to put the gold that he bought under his bed. It was never stolen, but there was always violence and robbery on the goldfield, and horse-stealing was endemic. Vigilance committees reinforced the

largely ineffectual police, but if this enforcement came close at times to lynch law, it was never to the extent that prevailed on the remote Queensland fields.

There was always the danger of miners being bailed up on the way to deposit their gold with the Commissioner, particularly if they had to come in from outlying diggings. Some preferred to hold on to their gold, rather than sell it at Kiandra and they tried to hide it in their calico huts and tents, or buried it. When they came to collect it, it was often to find it gone, which was the cue for yet more violence.

The greatest danger to the gold (though not to the miners, who had already been paid) came from bushrangers who bailed up the gold transports on their way to Sydney. The gold travelled under a heavy guard of mounted troopers known as the Gold Escort, but even the escort was vulnerable, and it was often waylaid. Negotiable banknotes could be cut in half and sent away in two different mails, but the gold itself had to be carried away and the cash brought in to pay for it.

Probably the fact that the rush was over so quickly ensured that the Assistant Commissioner's fears that Kiandra would become "a refugium of Victorian and New South Wales criminals", turned out to be unfounded. Even on the Victorian fields, where violence and mob rule were commonplace, there was seldom serious trouble in the first year. And the detested ticket-of-leave convicts from Tasmania—the Vandemonians—who terrorised the Victorian diggings, hardly made a mark at Kiandra.

The Bank of New South Wales set up shop on the diggings

at the very beginning of the rush and prided itself on having a calico tent "fully ten feet higher than the Oriental Bank on the other side of the street". A visitor making his first call at the bank found the second-in-command sitting on a piece of bark which rested on two logs. Running between the logs, in fact running right through the tent, was a stream of water which came from a thawing snow drift. The bank staff received no bonus for having to work in these conditions, and to supplement their meagre earnings they tried sinking a shaft inside the bank. Their initiative produced no gold.

Every gold town had its share of licensed—and unlicensed—grog shops and Kiandra was no exception, although the difficulty and expense of carting ale up the mountains meant that most sold only spirits.

Kidd's Exchange Hotel was the only place on the diggings where the miners could get a good, quick, hot meal. Kidd's was run by an American and the kitchen was supervised by a French chef (who prospered in Australia, then went to New Zealand where he was murdered). The restaurant was a long room with only one door, in the corner, to prevent the customers from slipping out without paying. The waiters doubled as bouncers and were often needed, and after the last meal had been served, the tables were cleared for gambling and at the end of the night, were used as shakedowns.

Down the street, the Empire Hotel, domain of a genial landlord called "Old Hoss" Carmichael, had a band, and wonder of wonders, three girls. Women of any kind at Kiandra for the first two years of the rush were a rarity and their time on the diggings must have been highly lucrative. In a room a little more than four metres by six, as many as 50 miners stood around smoking, drinking, eyeing the three girls and then usually dancing instead with each other. One of the more bizarre sights on the goldfields must have been 50 hefty miners, unshaven, grubby, their boots encrusted with dirt, dancing together on a floor an inch deep in mud.

As April eased into May, there was a perceptible sharpening in the weather, a chill reminder of what must shortly be expected. At the best of times Kiandra and the rolling, fog-shrouded hills around it can be bleak and inhospitable; in winter, with the temperature falling far below zero, and the bitter wind driving relentlessly, it can be almost unbearable.

For the miners, already huddling against the cold nights in their makeshift, calico-covered huts, which provided neither warmth against the cold nor protection against the rain, the prospect of the coming winter was daunting.

There were many stories of the ferocity of the Kiandra weather. In 1834, the high country experienced the worst blizzards on record and it was reported than when the snows melted the bodies of a mob of cattle were found hanging by their horns from the tops of snow gums. The following year, one man lost 300 cattle, reportedly smothered in the snow.

For many days each winter it snowed without respite, broken only by days of driving rain, and always that terrible, desolate wind, blowing unchecked through the bare hills. Most of the houses and other "buildings" were primitive. Two or three inns were built of wood, but the police still slept under a tent and the Gold Commissioner himself had an unlined calico shed, distinguishable from all the others only by its size.

Understandably, the official reports had concluded that fear of the approaching winter would drive all but a handful of the hardiest or most foolhardy miners out of Kiandra until the following spring, when the numbers on the field would swell to 150,000. "The place will become uninhabitable and unapproachable", the Gold Commissioner wrote to the Under Secretary on the approach of winter. As it turned out, the reports were wrong on both counts.

Contrary to all the predictions, some 3500 miners stayed to brave the winter, enduring the weather and working as best they could in the forbidding blizzards and rain, never growing used to the first miserable hours of each morning when the country was blanketed in a wet, freezing fog that reduced visibility to arm's length and brought on fits of violent shivering.

So bleak and windswept were the hills, that snow rarely drifted deeper than two metres in open country, even after the heaviest falls; but it was a different story when the snow encountered a solid object. The walls of the calico huts had to be constantly cleared of drifts to prevent them caving in under the weight, and they were always damp and cold.

The gold runs out

Somehow, the miners saw out the winter and managed to produce about 500 ounces of gold a week. The greatest danger turned out to be not the weather directly, but an acute shortage of food and then, when the springs froze over, of water. But when the storms finally abated and spring once more returned to the hills, it was clear that something far worse had happened. The gold was running out.

The main cause of the collapse at Kiandra was very simple: in spite of all the optimistic forecasts, the rich, shallow alluvial deposits had been worked out, the stream beds dredged, the nuggets all found. The reef gold was too hard to extract and there was just not enough gold to be found to keep the men on the field.

Two other factors certainly contributed to Kiandra's sudden death—the fear of having to endure another winter there and the discovery of good payable gold at Lambing Flat (today the site of Young). By March 1861, miners were abandoning the diggings in droves. By the end of the summer, barely 300 diggers remained and the Chinese soon outnumbered the Europeans. They seemed able to extract payable gold even from claims being worked for the third and fourth time.

On 11 February 1862, after the second winter, the surveyor's plan showed 62 buildings in Kiandra. Almost all were tenantless and falling rapidly into decay, walls flapping forlornly in the wind. By 1864, only two shops and two pubs could be found. Gradually, the few who had chosen to remain built more permanent buildings, better suited for surviving the bitter winters, and Kiandra took on the appearance of a compact little settlement of weatherboard homes, shops and hotels. The wives and families of some of the miners arrived to join them and tried to come to terms with the hardships of living and working in this desolate place.

Seven years after the rush, Kiandra opened its first school, though it does not seem to have been an unqualified success. In 1876, the Inspector of Schools paid a visit and reported, "Everything about this school is unsatisfactory. The building is bad, discipline of any effective kind can scarcely be said to exist and the attainments are wretched".

The area immediately around the Kiandra settlement was by no means the only part of the high country which produced payable gold. Prospectors fanned out through the hills in their quest, exploring uncharted rivers and streams, trudging over mountains and through the ravines. Some were well rewarded, notably at Four Mile and at Nine Mile and at Fifteen Mile, on the timbered ridge above the Tumut River.

Four Mile Hut (above) *was built in 1937 by Bob Hughes, the last active miner in the mountains and son of the famous skiing mailman of Kiandra. Today it is the only intact miner's dwelling on the Kiandra goldfields.*

(opposite) *A relic of the grazing days at Kiandra.*

Banjo Paterson's High Country

🐎 *The old cemetery at Kiandra is a stark reminder of the reality of the gold rush days and is a forlorn sight today. It is believed that some headstones were later used as blocks for kneading dough at the Kiandra bakery. Several of the Chinese graves were dug up in later years and the bones sent home to China.*

The Four Mile rush (it was four miles from Kiandra) occurred towards the end of January 1860 and a thousand diggers were soon working there, a surprising number of them making their fortunes. Nine Mile, too, produced excellent gold and kept another thousand men occupied.

Even within a comparatively small area, the nature of the gold varied considerably. At Tumut, for example, it was described as being "of a rich character and far superior to that of Kiandra", while that found in Snowy Plain was said to have "a very beautiful appearance, though of light weight". It all fetched the same price, however, between £3.7.4d and £3.11.11d according to the silver content in it. There was always some silver alloyed with the gold— sometimes as much as 7.7 per cent—which could not be separated on the goldfield.

Today, almost all trace of these mines has disappeared unless you look very closely. Nine Mile still has its surprises—huge earthworks, collapsed tunnels, the ruins of huts and, unexpectedly among the snow gums, an old two-seater dunny and an ancient cast-iron stove. Four Mile has one of the last intact miner's dwellings still standing on the entire Kiandra goldfields, a restored patchwork of flattened tins, slabs, glass and split boards.

Hydraulic sluicing was probably the first direct use of power from the waters of the Snowy Mountains. In California, where it was widely used before it was brought to Australia, legislation had to be introduced to ban it altogether, so devastating was the damage caused by millions of tonnes of tailings being washed into the rivers. In the fragile streams and rivers of the Australian high country, there was never any attempt at control and the evidence is still there 100 years later.

The sluicing process used powerful jets of water to break down the banks of the rivers and streams. The soil was then washed in lines of sluices to extract the gold. It required enormous amounts of water and many kilometres of pipes and aqueducts to get the water there. At first small dams, and then much larger dams were built on many of the streams, and from these, canals or races, sometimes several kilometres long, carried the water to a point above the workings. There it was passed through a series of progressively narrowing pipes into huge nozzles whose high pressure jets of water could cut away sixty tonnes of overburden in an hour.

Three Mile Dam, on the road to Tumut, almost opposite the turn-off to Mount Selwyn, was built for sluicing and is a good indicator of the amount of water that was needed. The dam holds 436 million gallons, or almost two billion litres. In all, there are more than 200 kilometres of race lines around Kiandra and all were built with pick and shovel or bullock-drawn plough.

There were two serious attempts to resurrect the diggings, in the 1880s, when hydraulic sluicing gouged deep craters out of the escarpment; and again during the depression of the 1930s when mining was more mechanised. But the old levels of gold were never found again and Kiandra's decline was never reversed.

Regular mining continued at Kiandra until 1905, after which no more than twenty miners ever worked the diggings at a time (apart from during the depression). The figures tell the story all too graphically. In the first year of the rush, the Kiandra field officially produced 67,687 ounces of gold, and in reality much more. In the second year, production was already down to 16,565 ounces, and over the next 75 years, a total of only 87,748 ounces was extracted. After 1937, no gold production at all was recorded and by 1949, Kiandra, which had promised so much, was virtually a ghost town.

In the years following the first rush, however, Kiandra was not entirely desolate. A school opened and the houses took on a more permanent appearance, and then tourists started to come. It was here that skiing had its beginnings in Australia. By 1905, the tourists were coming from Sydney, taking the train to Cooma, then an old-fashioned stage coach to Adaminaby. They covered the last 14 kilometres to Kiandra as best they could, which usually meant going on skis, whatever their experience, with the baggage strapped to their backs. In the teeth of a raging westerly gale, with no bonding on their skis except a single leather toe-strap, it must have been an unforgettable way for novices to start their holiday.

That skiing in Australia began here was understandable, considering that it was the first community in the country to be regularly snowbound for long periods each year (winters then were far more severe than today and the snow was much deeper). What is very unexpected is that the

Kiandra Snow-shoe Club was almost certainly the first ski club in the world, older even than the acknowledged first, the Oslo Ski Club, which was founded in 1877. Among the Snow-shoe Club's members were the marvellous pioneering Australian photographer, Charles Kerry, who was born on the Monaro and Banjo Paterson himself.

There was no skiing at all during the first winter of 1860. Perhaps the miners were too busy just surviving, or perhaps there wasn't a stick of wood available to make their skis, their "snow-shoes" as they called them. But by the end of the second winter, skiing was all the rage.

The diggers who had remained tore up the fences, turned up the tips of palings and began to ski. It was probably a Swede who did it first, but it was the fearlessness of the Norwegian miners that most appealed to the other diggers. One miner wrote in a letter of "the astounding way in which Norwegian semi-drunk miners would hurl themselves down slopes and over banks". He added, almost as an afterthought, that there were a lot of broken collar bones.

By "riding the shoes", as they called it, on the long mountain ash skis which quickly replaced the fencing, they travelled for miles. They skied to the diggings, through deep drifting snow and over snow that was frozen hard. They raced for money and just for the fun of it. And they skied to bring in the mail and take out the sick.

It was at about this time that the New South Wales Premier, Sir Joseph Carruthers, who loved the high country, decided to make it more accessible. The government built a very large hotel on Diggers Creek, the Hotel Kosciusko (which later burnt down); and another called the Creel, for fishermen, on the Thredbo River. It also replaced an old bullock track along the Ramshead Range from Charlotte's Pass to the summit of Kosciusko with a proper road.

For Kiandra, the opening of the Hotel Kosciusko in 1909 spelt the end of its brief life as a ski resort. It was the Main Range, with its steeper slopes and greater appeal as a winter resort, that would attract the huge investment needed to transform the unspoilt range into a multi-million dollar industry. There was nothing left over for Kiandra.

Today the town scarcely exists. One of the last remaining buildings, once the stone courthouse and later a hotel, is reduced to being used as a depot for the Main Roads Department. Once the houses were left empty, they soon

fell into disrepair. Many were lined with newspapers, layer upon layer—to keep out the wind and to provide reading matter on the long winter nights—and the goats (every family had a herd of goats) loved the taste of the sweet flour paste used as wallpaper glue. Any timber was quickly taken, and even flat stones in the chimneys were used for rough paths.

Many of the houses were held under Miners' Right and the men had the right to live in them for only as long as they were legally working a claim. Even those who owned the title to the land on which their houses stood knew that it was an almost worthless asset, and they simply abandoned them when they left the goldfield.

In spring a bed of daffodils, absurd in the setting of the decayed town, makes a bold show of yellow, and in mid-summer lupins flower in profusion. In the little cemetery on the hill above Permanent Creek, the Chinese were segregated from the Europeans, or perhaps the other way around. Most of their remains were later dug up and sent back to China.

The grave stones that have survived the vandals and the cruel winters, are being eroded by the passing years. Still almost unbearably pathetic are the tiny graves, some unmarked, of the children who were left behind in that lonely place.

The road to Three Mile Dam is there, with its two hills called Gentle Annie and Roaring Meg. No one can remember Gentle Annie, but Roaring Meg lived with Brandy Mary at the Three Mile and after a night at the pub in Kiandra, the two of them would head for home on foot. As they staggered up the steep hill, Meg could be heard roaring into the night three miles back in Kiandra!

You feel there should be more to see in a place that once was home to 15,000 red-blooded miners, all intent on finding their fortune in gold. Where was the bank, its clerk sitting aside a stream as the snowdrift melted against the back wall of his calico hut? Where did the school stand where discipline no longer existed and attainments were wretched? And where was Old Hoss's Empire Hotel, where 50 miners shared three girls and danced with each other instead?

There are no clues on the ground. Just ghosts when the wind howls down from those bleak and cheerless hills and winter closes in with slanting rain and unkind snow.

Stamper battery and other gold mining equipment are on display at the foot of the most productive gold-bearing claim, New Chum Hill.

The Snowy Mountains

Of all the earth's great land masses, Australia is among the least mountainous. Some 450 million years ago, much of what is now eastern Australia was covered by a great sea and the land that we know as the Kosciusko region lay under the water. Remnants of the sediments of this sea can still be seen as the slates and quartzites between Rawson's Pass, near the summit of Mount Kosciusko, and Watson's Crags.

For millions of years, the earth's crust folded and lifted under the sea, while sedimentation continued to pile up until eventually it rose above the level of the water. Granite intruded and gradually a region of mountains and high country was formed. Then, over the next 60 million years, there was a period of stability in the earth's crust and at the same time, weathering slowly wore down the hills and mountains almost to sea level. Only a few of the most resistant parts, including some of the present day Kosciusko peaks, remained above the level of the plain.

About 65 million years ago, at the beginning of the geological time span known as the Tertiary Period, there was another series of more gradual upheavals, which again raised up much of eastern Australia, creating the Great Dividing Range. Finally, late in the Tertiary, a massive fault developed and a great slab of land which included almost the whole of the Australian Alps, tipped up on one side in what became known as the Kosciusko Uplift.

Streams that had meandered sluggishly across the peneplain became swift rivers as the plain tilted upwards at one end, and gouged their way into the rock, to form great canyons and gulleys. Fractures in the rocks provided weak areas where some of these rivers were able to cut down and form the long, straight parallel courses that we can see today in the Crackenback, Upper Snowy, Guthega and Munyang Rivers.

For most of the Tertiary, the climate was warmer and wetter than it is now, which we can see in the fossil record, but about two million years ago the world began to cool. At higher latitudes and altitudes glaciers developed, then disappeared during warmer interglacial periods, only to recur as the earth cooled again. At least four Ice Ages affected Australia, although all appear to have been weak; and the cirques, mountain lakes, moraines and erratics—large rocks carried over a long distance by the glaciers and then dumped when the glacier retreated—all date from these periods.

For the last few thousand years, Kosciusko, and indeed the whole continent, has been all but ice-free, even though some snow patches can still persist for more than a year. It has been argued that the Kosciusko region is at the very end of the last Ice Age, which occurred only 10,000

(opposite) *Rolling snow drifts on the main range.*

(above) *Cascades Hut.*

The Snowy Mountains

The Sentinel (left), *the Kosciusko Summit* (below) and *Watson's Crags* (bottom) *are remnants of a 400 million year-old mountain range worn by the ravages of time.*

(top) *The Alpine Anenome*—Ranunculus anemoneus.
(centre) *Billy buttons*—craspedia.
(bottom) *Gunn's Willow-herb.*

years ago. Certainly, there is much less snow, and winters are far less severe today than they were even half a century ago. Fifty years, of course, is too short a time in normal circumstances for any such change to manifest itself; but the presence of enormous expanses of water in the new man-made reservoirs, such as Lake Eucumbene and Lake Jindabyne, may have unnaturally accelerated the final days of the Ice Age.

The Great Dividing Range—an odd misnomer, for nowhere is it great, and rarely is it even recognisable as a range—forms the shape of the letter N as it passes through the Australian Alps. The left leg, the Snowy Mountains themselves, stretches northwards from the Victorian border; and then at Rules Point, near the Yarrangobilly Caves, it turns abruptly to run south-east, down along the Monaro Range, through Bradley's old properties, Coolringdon and Myalla, until it reaches Nimmitabel. There it makes another abrupt turn, this time once more to the north, and heads off towards the Blue Mountains, the next great barrier on the Divide.

Because the mountains and their plains are tilted, like a massive wedge, the approach to some of the peaks from the east is little more than a leisurely stroll. With none is this more so than Kosciusko. It is the western face that is dramatic, with its sweeping amphitheatre of mountains marking the edge of the plateau. Beyond, the slopes fall away steeply into deep gorges and jagged ravines, and the view from the summit is across the Geehi Gorge and the Murray, far into Victoria. On cloudy, misty mornings an immense sea of cloud fills every valley, the peaks jutting up like so many islands.

The uniqueness of the Australian Alps does not lie in their height—the tallest of them all, Mount Kosciusko is only 2228 metres above sea level, and much less above the surrounding plain. The Welsh would call these mountains hills, and that would not be to belittle them, for they are lovely, lonely places, as wild and desolate at times and as warm and enticing as any on earth.

They can be treacherous, too, in punishing those rash enough to take them for granted, blowing up a storm of great fury from a flawless, blue sky or a leaden winter afternoon. The suddenness and the ferocity of the storms in these mountains is frightening. Sometimes soft, heavy snowflakes are drifting down without a whisper of a breeze, sometimes there isn't even the smallest cloud in the sky—when suddenly, without any apparent warning, the full fury of the wind, driving horizontally into your face, strikes without warning.

Dense clouds of snow begin to swirl across the hills as the rising wind tears at clothes and skin. In minutes, the sun has dimmed to the palest of yellow orbs and then goes out. Direction becomes meaningless because the wind seems to be coming from every direction at once. In such conditions, it is wise to stop, huddle into whatever protection can be found, and attempt to ride out the storm.

At last, often as suddenly and dramatically as it began, the storm that has been moaning through the rocks, blows itself out and there is an intense stillness, a moment of such relief that the temptation to shout out loud is overwhelming. And there are moments, too, of such beauty that one holds one's breath, fearful that any movement will break the spell. Such a moment comes when the clouds part and the sun streams through, as though through the skylight of some great abbey, and lights up the very peak of a mountain. Then this too passes and the day, exhausted, makes way for night.

There are warnings of these storms, if you only know where to look for them. The animals and birds sense them. At Kiandra, the miners used to know when to batten down for a storm when the mice began running up and down the curtains. When a flock of screeching yellow-tailed black cockatoos is seen flying purposefully towards the east, that too means that wild weather is no more than 24 hours away. And the old prospectors used to reckon that only a fool would venture out when Jagungal's summit was shrouded in cloud or mist.

Winter mists and fogs are always frightening. Mist at sea is grey, but this mist is of the purest white, blinding in its brightness, and it can leave a man with a sense of foreboding and helplessness that is matched by no other in the hills. Shapes and outlines are magnified and distorted, so that the boulders of the moraines, weird at any time, become grotesque. Climbers swear they have seen men eleven feet tall in the mountain fogs, and always there is the fear that one false step will send you plunging down the side of the mountain into what your imagination tells you is an invisible abyss on every side.

The two highest peaks, Kosciusko and Townsend, are about as different as any two mountains in the entire Main Range. (The names Main Range and Snowy Mountains are usually used indiscriminately.) They rise only about four kilometres from each other and they are linked by an old bridle track.

Kosciusko is rounded with gentle slopes and its shape suggests that it was smoothed by a rolling sheet of ice. Townsend, on the other hand, is a far more impressive mountain, its summit not rounded at all, but rocky and craggy. For some reason, this mountain, but not Kosciusko, was a nunatak, a peak that sticks up above the ice sheet in glacial times and so becomes weathered and broken, not smooth and rounded.

From Kosciusko, there are magnificent views in every direction, but from the summit the sides of the mountain fall away gradually. From Townsend, almost from the base of the trig point, the mountain's sides go tumbling away down to the valleys of the Geehi River and Swampy Plain River more than 1800 metres below.

At the far end of the Townsend Spur is Mt Alice Rawson, itself one of the highest peaks in the range, and from its summit one has a magnificent view down into Lady Northcote's Canyon and the Geehi Gorge, and a panorama right across to Watson's Crags.

A little further along the range is the Sentinel, a sinister little mountain, dark and portentous when it is in the shadow of Carruthers late in the afternoon, or on a gloomy, overcast day. Deep chasms separate the Sentinel from Watson's Crags and Townsend Spur, the most precipitous of all the ridges of the Main Range.

The flora of the high country is so special because it blooms in such profusion and in so many species there,

After the snow melt in spring, the mountains are transformed with carpets of wildflowers in every imaginable hue. Most of the 250 species found in the high country are unique to the region. Even on the most exposed slopes and feldmark delicate blooms weather the worst of the storms.

Banjo Paterson's High Country

and for its unparalleled loveliness. After the snow melts in spring and early summer, the mountains are transformed as whole hillsides erupt in a mass of colour of every imaginable hue. On a clear morning, the fragrance of the flowers is so heady that it is intoxicating and the wonder is that many of these flowers are unique in Australia—perhaps 250 species are found nowhere else on the continent.

Even on the most exposed slopes, at the very peaks of the mountains, or on that marvellous ecosystem known as feldmark, there are shrubs and flowers bravely weathering the worst of the storms. There are only ten hectares of feldmark, with its minute shrubs and the tiniest of flowers, throughout the mountains. On the cruellest of the slopes, only the heaths manage to survive, like the tough little Snow heath (*Epacris petrophila*), and the curious Coral heath (*E. microphylla*) which has taken survival to its limits. These little heart-shaped leaves and clusters of white flowers survive only on the leeward side of the plant.

The aromatic Alpine Mint-bush (*Prostanthera cuneata*) blooms profusely through the summer, high in the mountains, its white and pale violet flowers a lovely contrast to the dark green leaves. It is the leaves, incidentally, not the flowers which smell so strongly.

Among the first flowers to appear after the snow melts are the buttercups (*Ranunculus spp*) and the high country can claim both the largest and smallest of the buttercups. The biggest and surely the most showy of them all is white Anemone buttercup (*R.anemoneus*), once grazed almost to extinction, but now, since the cattle were barred from the high country in New South Wales, making a spectacular recovery so that they are almost the most abundant of all the high country flowers.

The tiny Dwarf buttercup (*R.millanii*) has the remarkable ability to survive for long periods completely submerged. It is one of the delights of walking in this beautiful country to come upon a stream cascading down the side of a hill and look into the water to see this exquisite little cream-coloured flower in full bloom beneath the water.

R.millanii begins to develop while it is still covered by the snow, which allows it to be one of the first of all the flowers to bloom when the snow melts; and another flower which has become highly specialised in much the same way is the Alpine Marsh-marigold (*Caltha introloba*), which is

considered to be a very primitive close relative of the Ranunculus family. It is sweetly perfumed and its very varied flowers and bright green leaves not only grow in wet, cold snow patches, but actually start to open under the snow. Indeed, it appears to need this covering of snow to bloom successfully.

The little Alpine Rice-flower (*Pimelea alpina*), its dainty pink buds followed by creamy white flowers, is another plant that is early to flower; and a little later, perhaps the most spectacular of all for their sheer profusion over whole hillsides of the mountains, are the meadows of daisies, the Brachychomes and Celmisias.

For many, the flower that they remember longest is the silver Snow daisy (*Celmisia spp*), its silvery blue-green leaves and masses of white flowers carpeting endless hectares of the country throughout the summer, sometimes so densely that they more resemble snowdrifts than fields of flowers.

The unique faces of the Snowy Mountains— the almost sunburnt appearance of the mountain eucalypts, the crystal clear rivers and mountain streams and the constantly changing weather.

There is another daisy, less prolific, but certainly no less lovely, the Brachychome nivalis, which prefers steep, rocky habitats.

The exquisite Mountain gentian (*Gentianella diemensis*), with white and cream delicate crocus-like flowers, blooms rather late, in February and March, and comes out with another delight, the Bluebell (*Wahlenbergia spp*).

Then there are the lovely balls of yellow and golden Craspedia, the Billy-buttons, patchworking the hills, and some spectacular everlastings, like the Alpine Sunray (*Helipterum albicans subsp. alpinum*), with orange and yellow-centred papery white flowers and silvery, woolly leaves; and the true everlastings, the Helichrysums — the papery, golden - yellow Button everlastings (*H. scorpioides*), and the highly perfumed Cascade ever-lastings (*H. secundiflorum*), with parchmenty, creamy - white flowers.

The Helichrysums include the interesting *H. hokkeri*, known as the kerosene bush because of its flammability. Like many of the wattles, it is highly adapted to fire and recovers spectacularly.

Most of the orchids which grow so magnificently in the sub-Alpine woodlands, do not extend above the treeline; but in the highest hills you may come across the Mauve Leek-orchid (*Prasophyllum suttonii*).

Almost all the trees in the high country are eucalypts, with occasional natives of the Callitris species. On the lower mountain slopes, the eucalypts of the dry sclerophyll forests—red stringy-barks, candle barks and broad-leaved peppermints—predominate, their thick, leathery leaves specially adapted to retain moisture.

There are still stands of the enormous mountain ash, soaring to 85 metres and more and one of the most spectacular trees in the world. Its crown of creamy blossom

Banjo Paterson's High Country

The Snow Gum (Eucalyptus niphophila) *is a hardy tree, growing where no other trees can survive.*

and sun-baked leaves fills the air for miles around with its pungent aroma. One of the most magnificent stands is on the slopes above the Indi River, between Pack Saddle Gap and the Cascades.

White sallee and black sallee grow in many parts of the high country, the black an important timber for the settlers. It was known once as green gum, from its chlorophyll-rich bark, but much better as muzzlewood, although the reason for the name is already fading from memory. In the days before the widespread use of fencing, it was not possible to wean calves by physically separating them from their mothers, so the settlers carved muzzles from black sallee which allowed the calf to eat grass, but not to lift its head to suck.

It is the snow gum, though, which is indelibly associated with the high country and the mountains. It is one of the loveliest and strangest of all the eucalypts, its trunk becoming more tortured and stunted the nearer the tree-line it grows—some are 400 years old and less than five metres tall. The beautiful colours, a kaleidoscope of yellows, greens, silver, pink and deepest red, are acquired from the tree's habit of peeling in thin strips over several years. As it peels, the trunk is exposed and then gradually changes

colour as it returns over the years to the new bark and begins the whole process all over again. Candlebark does much the same thing, but because it sheds all its bark at the same time in the one year, it lacks the marvellous variety of the snow gum.

The first Europeans to see the Snowy Mountains were probably Hume and Hovell, in 1824, as they forced their way down Tumbarumba Creek while exploring from Lake George through to Bass Strait. They suddenly came across a view of snowy mountains ahead of them, much higher than the ubiquitous forest and set against the bluest of skies.

Hovell wrote, "a prospect came in View the most Magnificeant, this was an immence highe Mountain Covered nearly one fourth of the way down with Snow, and the Sun shining upon it gave it a most brilliant appearance." This was in spite of the fact that it was springtime and hot.

Another diary entry by a member of the party recorded that "the sight of this mountain range, rising out of the blue skies . . . was such that the men's exclamations drew the others of their party running."

Paul Edmund de Strzelecki has always been given credit for being the first European to get to the top of the continent's highest mountain, and perhaps he was. Strzelecki (perhaps after having what they believed to be the highest mountain pointed out to him by the Pendergasts), went up what became known as Hannel's Spur, a very steep climb on the western side of the range. He reached the summit on 15 February 1840 and named the mountain Kosciusko after a celebrated Polish patriot.

The only fly in the ointment is that Strzelecki had almost certainly climbed the wrong mountain and reached the summit not of Kosciusko, but of Townsend. Townsend is a far more impressive peak and climbing up the way that he had done, it would have seemed higher than Kosciusko. (It is actually 18 metres lower.)

That he did make a mistake is borne out by Strzelecki's own diary which read for that day, "the view from its summit sweeps over 7000 square miles . . . Beneath the feet, looking from the very verge of the cone downwards, almost perpendicularly, the eye plunges into a fearful gorge 3000 feet deep, in the bed of which, sources of the Murray gather their contents and roll their united waters to the west".

That is an almost exact description of the view from the summit of Townsend and not remotely like that from Koscuisko. What happened then is largely conjecture. According to James Macarthur, who had financed the trip and who went with Strzelecki, the Pole realised his mistake and immediately took two Aboriginals and crossed to Kosciusko so that he really could claim to be the first to the top of the highest mountain.

It does seem most peculiar, to say the least, that if this is what really happened, Strzelecki made no mention of it and described only his visit to the top of a mountain from whose summit his eye plunged 1800 metres vertically down into the Geehi River far below. (Macarthur in his own diary had described "struggling" up to the summit, which would be likely on Townsend, extremely unlikely on Kosciusko.)

There is a great temptation to believe that Macarthur, having financed the whole expedition, might have been very reluctant to return to Sydney and admit that they actually climbed the wrong mountain. And if indeed he knew of the mistake before he returned to England, Strzelecki, with his background, might very well have preferred to remain silent.

Strzelecki had a most unlikely background for an explorer who would later be honoured by two of the most prestigious societies in the world. A Pole, he left school without matriculating, entered the Prussian army and then tried unsuccessfully to elope. Thwarted in love, he decided to head for London, but he left Poland under suspicion of having embezzled, either to finance his elopement or his plans for getting over its failure.

In 1833, he had arrived in London, introduced himself as a count, which he was not, and set about living on a minuscule income and an immense amount of charm. He travelled in the Americas and the Pacific Islands, studying earth sciences, then went to New Zealand and finally arrived in Sydney in 1839, where he began work on a geological map.

The Alpine Way wends its way down the mountain to Khancoban, where it meets the Murray River, dividing New South Wales and Victoria.

Banjo Paterson's High Country

Later, when he returned to England, he would receive recognition that he can only have dreamed of, awarded fellowships of the Royal Society and the Royal Geographical Society, an honorary degree from Oxford and, surely the ultimate prize for a man who had invented the title of count for himself, a knighthood.

Macarthur's diary was not publicly disclosed until 1942 and may simply have been kept by Macarthur as insurance in case he was ever challenged on the point.

The problem was enormously complicated because for many years, local bushmen called Townsend, Kosciusko; the whole Main Range was sometimes referred to as Kosciusko; and Mount Kosciusko appeared on official maps for many years as Townsend!

Names throughout the high country are a worry to any geographer. The early European settlers were there for many reasons, and they were very likely to go about their business without meeting anyone else. Maps were few and far between, so each of them gave their own names to the rivers and mountains and the places where they camped.

Perisher Mountain was named by James Spencer when he went over the top in a gale while he was searching for stray cattle, and was almost blown off his horse by the icy blast that hit him. And Mount Paralyser was named shortly afterwards when they went over another hill, and Spencer's stockman grumbled, "If the last one was Perisher, then this is a Paralyser!" Disappointment Spur and Devil's Staircase surely got their names in much the same way.

(above) *Early morning dew on a spiders web.*

The Snow Gum is the only tree to grow on the windswept hills above 1800 metres. Its gnarled trunk and branches, weighed down by snow during the winter, burst forth with the sweetest cream-coloured blossom and wax-coated gumnuts during the warmer months.

Sometimes they used the Aboriginal name—or at least what they thought the Aboriginals were saying which caused endless confusion. The Aboriginal name for Kosciusko itself was Targan-gil, but the meaning has long since been lost.

Whatever the truth about Strzelecki, he may not have been the first European to reach the summit in any case (always assuming that the Pendergasts or some other stockmen had not been there without realising the significance of it).

Strzelecki's fellow-countryman, John Lhotsky, claimed that it was *he* who had first climbed the highest mountain. He called it Mount William IV, but there is increasing suspicion that he too had not climbed Kosciusko, and instead went up Mount Terrible, south of the Crackenback.

Lhotsky was a trained scientist—he had been educated as a doctor and a naturalist—and certainly should have had the knowledge to calculate the height of the mountain, yet no one could conceivably describe Terrible as "the highest mountain in Australia", as Lhotsky did in his diary. His route is hard to follow, because some of the pages of his diary are missing (or were never written) and he was not a careful diarist.

In fact, his life was a series of disasters. He had been given a grant to mount a natural history expedition to South America and Australia, but he arrived in Sydney in 1832 and tried without success to get a job with a museum. Eventually, in 1834 and still without a sponsor—his grant had long since run out—he went off to explore the Snowy Mountains. He was six years ahead of Strzelecki. He did publish an incomplete account of his journey, which he titled *Journey from Sydney to the Australian Alps*, but to survive he sold vegetables and firewood to the squatters.

From every account, Lhotsky's main problem throughout his life seemed to have been himself. He appears to have been so tactless and rude in Australia that he was unable to find a job, and when he finally sailed for England in 1838 he was still only 38. Whereas Strzelecki was showered with honours, Lhotsky, far better educated, received no recognition at all. He sank into poverty and died destitute in 1861.

Perhaps the truth is that neither Lhotsky nor Strzelecki climbed Kosciusko when they said they did, and that the first ascent was indeed made by the stockmen. No one in the mountains would object if that turned out to be the case.

Tarns and mountain lakes

One of the delights of walking in the mountains is coming unexpectedly upon a lake high in the Main Range—not one of the great flooded valleys of the hydro-electric scheme, but an icy waterhole, a remnant of the last Ice Age. In hollows and beds gouged out of the rock by the ice, most are retained by terminal moraines of boulders and debris dumped by the glaciers when the warming climate halted them in their tracks and they began to melt and recede back up the valleys.

There are five of these enchanting lakes, the largest of them, Blue Lake, covering only 16 hectares, the smallest, Club Lake, just a tenth of that size. Within the memory of a few, there was once a sixth as well, a little tarn between Townsend and Mount Alice Rawson at the far end of Townsend Spur. It was called Russell Tarn (a tarn is a small mountain lake), after the government meteorologist of the day, or Lake Claire, and when it existed, it was the highest waterhole in Australia.

It was apparently much warmer than the other lakes, not as the legend has it, because it had a secret, warm spring bubbling in its bed, but because the dark brown peat bottom and sides absorbed the sun's heat and warmed the water. Probably for no reason more complicated than the amount of snow in this area has lessened over the years, it dried up and today this lake has completely vanished.

Blue Lake is, for many, the most perfect of lakes. It is also the deepest, more than 25 metres deep at one point. Although it has a moraine at one end, this plays only a small part in damming it, for it lies in a deep bed that was gouged out of the rock by the erosive weight of three converging valley glaciers.

It is only on cloudless days that the lake is blue. When the sky is grey and leaden and the clouds are full of snow, it is bleak and unwelcoming; and when the gales howl through the mountains, it becomes a dangerous place for any small craft venturing on to its surface, as Professor Edgeworth David did nearly 90 years ago, in a little hand-made coracle, to plumb its chilly depths for the first time.

The slippery snowgrass on the great mass of Little Twynam, towering above the lake, is treacherous after rain, and in winter massive green-blue icicles hang suspended from the rocks, and innumerable waterfalls tumble down the granite face of the mountain. It is a magical place in winter, utterly silent, the water frozen hard and covered with a layer of soft snow across which the occasional skiers glide, as though over an immense skating rink.

Lake Albina, surrounded by the precipitous walls of Lady Northcote's Canyon (opposite), *and morning light over Club Lake, the smallest of the five lakes near Mount Kosciusko* (above).

Tarns and mountain lakes

The water from Blue Lake runs away in Blue Lake Creek, into the more modest and much shallower Hedley Tarn only half a kilometre further downstream. The valley below Blue Lake is filled with an extraordinary moraine of enormous, almost unclimbable boulders, abandoned in total disarray by the retreating glacier. To come on Helms Moraine, as it is known, half-hidden in a winter mist, is an eerie and unsettling experience.

Below the shining cliffs of Mount Carruthers is the smallest of the lakes, the delightful little Club Lake which was given its name because it resembled the club-shaped cattle brand of a local grazier. It is fed by a little stream that rushes into the lake and then emerges at the far end to tumble on down to the valley below, in a series of waterfalls and crystal pools. In spring and summer, its banks are a mass of the loveliest moisture-loving plants. The lake is only two metres deep because of heavy silting, and again because of the silt, only a sixth of its original depth and half its size in area.

For some, the most perfect lake of all is Albina, surrounded by the precipitous walls of Lady Northcote's Canyon plunging to the Geehi Gorge, 1200 metres below. Albina is unusual in that it does not lie in a cirque at the head of a glacial valley, but in a hollow scooped out of the valley bed by the glacier. Again because of silting, it is much shallower at the southern end than the northern, and it is almost divided in two by a granite ridge. The waters are held in place by a classic terminal moraine across the valley and the water from the outlet falls immediately down into the canyon.

Only a kilometre from the summit of Kosciusko, nestling in a little valley to the south of the mountain, is the quaintly named Lake Cootapatamba, "the lake where eagles drink", in Aboriginal. Like Hedley Tarn it is a shallow lake; but unlike Hedley, it is a remnant of a much larger glacial lake that once spread across the valley of the Upper Swampy Plains River. It is fed from the snows of the Cootapatamba Drift, an immense snow drift that forms on the eastern shoulder of Kosciusko, where snow 21 metres deep, the deepest ever recorded in the high country, was encountered one year.

Lake Cootapatamba nestles at the southern end of Mount Kosciusko (left).

(above) *Icy waters of Blue Lake, the largest and deepest of the glacial lakes.*

Jagungal, the Big Bogong

Rising from the swamp like a great white ghost, Jagungal, mantled in the snow of a heavy winter, is a breathtaking sight. In spring and summer, when the snows have gone, it is the most unmistakable of all the peaks, its rocky summit a great crouching lion silhouetted against the empty sky.

It is not Jagungal's height that makes it so impressive—it is 167 metres lower than Kosciusko—so much as its isolation. It seems to stand alone and stark in the plain, towering over the Bogong Swamp, dominating the horizon no matter from where it is viewed. The melting snows and water courses on Jagungal feed the Murray and the Tumut and a dozen other streams.

It is a mountain of moods, not unrelievedly sinister like the Sentinel, nor awesome and bleak like Townsend or Watson's Crags. Rather, it mirrors the light, the sky and the clouds, one moment beguiling and lovely, the next dark and forbidding.

It is a rocky mountain, but in winter the rocks are concealed beneath the snow and ice. At the summit, ice caves form between them, picturesque but deceptive, offering scant protection to anyone unwary enough to be caught unprepared by a blizzard howling in across the plain, unchecked, from the clearest of blue skies. And when cloud and mist settle over the mountain like a shroud, it is a sure sign that foul weather is close behind.

Yet it is the summit that is irresistibly alluring, for on a clear day the view must surely be the most beautiful in all Australia, as far as the eye can see in every direction, for more than 100 kilometres when other mountains do not intervene, and over as many peaks. To the west, far beyond the Dargals and across the Murray Valley, lies Victoria; to the east are the Munyang Mountains, "munyang" the Aboriginal word for enormous; while to the south are the great cliffs and gorges of the Main Range, and Kosciusko itself, from whose own summit Jagungal's lion irresistibly draws the eye.

Jagungal was first officially climbed by miners from Grey Mare, just before the turn of the century, but others must surely have scrambled to its summit before that. Having once seen this view, it seems inconceivable that they would not have been drawn back there again. Nor is it a difficult climb from the west in the spring and summer.

The old-time skiers quickly discovered Jagungal. They raced down the glacier-like western slope towards Rocky Plains Creek, riding their brake-sticks like hobby-horses, or showing off by tackling the two-kilometre run down to the river at great speed, with no sticks at all, crouching low, one ski slightly ahead of the other.

Mount Jagungal, known to the stockmen as the Big Bogong, after the bogong moths which come in their millions each summer. O'Keefes Hut (Bogong Hut) is tucked in the western lee of Jagungal.

Banjo Paterson's High Country

Legend has it that a man can sink from sight in the Bogong Swamp, sucked down by the spongey sphagnum bog. It isn't true, but there are some who tread cautiously for all that. In spring, the plain and the marsh and the mountain itself are a lovely patchwork of flowers, of yellow Alpine bottlebrush, purple milkwort and the delicate sky-blue of the waxy bluebells which smell so sweetly when they are dried, the smell of newly mown hay.

The bluebells flower late in the season, in February and March, as do the strange pink and red and purple Grass trigger-plants. Their columns bent back, cocked and ready to fire, they are an ingenious booby-trap designed to perpetuate the species, springing forward and spraying their pollen on any insect that lands on them. Firing the trigger-plant with a piece of grass or a twig is a game that every child of the bush has played.

Amongst the bright yellow - green cushions of moss in the swamp, sweet - scented heaths thrive in the wet soil. Here and there looking somehow lost and out of place in this carpet of soft pastel colours, glows the brilliance of a sun orchid (*Thelmyra* spp). This lovely orchid takes its name from its habit of remaining closed except in strong sunlight.

Nobody knows what the word Jagungal means, nor indeed, if it really was the Aboriginal word for the mountain. The Aboriginals disappeared so fast after the Europeans arrived that tantalisingly little was recorded: much of what we do know was passed down by word of mouth, or often inaccurately committed to paper by people unskilled in their own language, let alone the strange sounds of the Aboriginal vocabulary and syntax. At one time Strzelecki called the mountain Mount Coruncal, then shortly afterwards, Mount Corunal.

If Jagungal was the correct Aboriginal name and Strzelecki simply misheard it repeated by a European, it was probably heavily accented on the first syllable which would explain why to local bushmen, it always was, and still is, "Jargonul". It is their shibboleth, their way of identifying their own kind from the interlopers and outsiders who call it, phonetically, "Jagungal".

But the mountain had another name and about the meaning of that, there is no doubt at all, for we have taken it into the Australian vocabulary. Long before white man arrived, the mountain to the Aboriginals was also Bogong, after the bogong moth, a prized delicacy.

The Aboriginals often named hills and mountains, streams and rivers, after a food especially associated with them. In consequence, there were numerous mountains just called Bogong. The Europeans tried to bring some order into this and added their own descriptive names, so today we have Little Bogong, Rocky Bogong with its pink granite, Dicky Cooper's Bogong after an Aboriginal who returned to the same place in search of the moths each year, Grey Mare Bogong which looks across the massive rift of the Geehi Gorge to the western face of the Main Range, and across the Murray, Victoria's highest mountain, Mount Bogong. And, of course, Jagungal itself, the Big Bogong.

The bogong moth, *Agrotis infusa*, is an unprepossessing looking creature that is no friend of the gardener. Drab brown and not very large, it is the adult stage of the pestiferous cut-worm. Each year the moths are compelled to migrate in their millions to the coolest place they can find, to escape the heat of summer, and nowhere in Australia is cooler than the topmost peaks of the mountains.

During the last ice age, they may have aestivated lower down the slopes, but as the glaciers melted and the high country warmed up, they moved higher and higher until they could go no further. There they gather in the caves and darkest crevices, usually on the western side of the granite peaks and just below the summit.

The first moths to arrive are greeted by the raucous cawing of the crows and the strange, mournful barking of the little ravens. They claim the deepest, darkest places. Then more moths pour in and tuck their heads under the wings of those already there, until they are stacked in layers, like tiles on a roof, sometimes 17,000 of them in an area of less than a square metre.

The Aboriginals arrived with the crows. They came from Yass and Braidwood, from Eden and Bega on the coast, and from Mitta Mitta and Omeo across the Murray. Mostly they seem to have been peaceable apart from the coastal and the Victorian tribes who squabbled whenever they met.

It was usually the men who caught the moths, using nets made from bark fibre. They cooked them in hollows of hot ash or took them back down the mountain to where their women were waiting, throwing them into the ashes and then winnowing off the legs and wings. Some of the moths were pounded into a paste by the women and baked into a cake.

The nutty-flavoured moths were so rich in fat and protein that eating them produced violent nausea until the system got used to them, but the Aboriginals feasted on them for months and they were nutritionally very important. Many of the Europeans described the Aboriginals as becoming sleek and very healthy after their sustained diet of bogong moth.

Sometimes the smoke from their cooking fires was so dense that surveyors wrote complainingly that they could no longer see the peaks to take their bearings; and the Aboriginal music, "plaintive and weird in the extreme", with bullroarers echoing off the rocks and through the ravines, was unsettling and frightening to many of the white settlers.

Towards the end of summer the moths become restless and by the time the first real storms of winter blew through the mountains, they had gone, and most of the Aboriginals with them. Sometimes the Aboriginals were caught by unexpected early storms, or by the unpredictable blizzards that can blow up even in summer. Sometimes they died, buried in the snow or overtaken by hypothermia in the bitter cold. Today, the bogongs still come to Jagungal, only now the crows and the ebony-black ravens feast on them alone.

The high country huts

The huts in the high country are a puzzle to those who are strangers to the mountains. They are uncomfortable and frequently overcrowded, the rats love them, and if some are unquestionably beautiful examples of bush craftsmanship, a good many are funny little buildings, knocked together with a bit of this and a bit of that. There is no immediate clue to the reason for the fury which is generated whenever anyone suggests that the huts have no place in a national park, let alone in a wilderness.

Understanding is helped by knowing how dangerous the high country can be. Almost all these huts originally existed for only one purpose, to shelter the men who had to work in this harsh environment. And it helps, too, to remember that the huts are almost the last tangible link with a part of the mountains' history that is already passing into folklore, a link with the old stockmen and brumby runners, with the men who mined the gold and the tin, and with the days when nearly every family could claim to have the original "Man from Snowy River" under its roof.

They are an odd collection of huts. Once they were scattered all through the high country, but today many are close to ruin and some have disappeared without a trace. None are alike and they vary in size from an entire homestead, abandoned when its run was absorbed by the park, to tiny huts which feel overcrowded when four people squeeze into them.

Because few were built with recreation in mind, the huts are dotted around in places that at first seem purposeless until their original function is remembered. They are never locked and so many lives have been saved by them, and so many lost because there was no hut within reach when it was needed, that it seems incomprehensible that anyone might want to remove them for the sake of appearance.

The huts are classified according to their importance, either for survival, recreation or historic and architectural value. More than forty of them are maintained by the Kosciusko Huts Association, a group of dedicated volunteers who "adopt" a hut and then devote hours to caretaking and preserving it and sometimes completely restoring it. They carry out their work with meticulous attention to detail, searching for materials as nearly identical to those in the original hut as they can find—even to the point of handmaking rivets and cutting off the heads of nails for greater authenticity. If building a replica of a hut that has been destroyed takes away something of its historical importance, it is more than compensated for by the unique opportunity to keep alive the skills of the bush carpenters and the other bush craftsmen.

Wheelers Hut, built at the turn of the century.

Sign on the slab walls of Oldfields Hut (above).

81

Banjo Paterson's High Country

These huts in the high country of Australia have nothing in common with their namesakes in Norway or the European Alps, many of which are comfortable, well-designed chalets. Among the European migrants who came to work on the Snowy scheme were many experienced skiers who very quickly saw the appeal of having a chain of lodges along the Main Range. Three were actually built before bureaucracy, the completion of the hydro-electric scheme and the total supremacy of downhill skiing over cross-country skiing in terms of allocation of funds, put the final nails in the coffin of what turned out to be no more than a clever idea.

🐎(above) *The chimney of Pockets Hut.*
(above right) *Oldfields Hut.*
(centre) *Yaouk Tin Hut.*
(below) *Bolton's Hut.*
(opposite) *The semi-derelict Teddys Hut.*

Albina Lodge, near Lake Albina, was the first to be built as a chalet, in 1951. It was advertised as a lodge for experienced skiers, complete with hot water, gas, 12-volt electricity and accommodation for 12 in two-bunk rooms. Albina lasted until 1983, although it had fallen into disuse years previously, when it was burnt down because the park management considered that it had become a health and environmental hazard. It simply became too popular and the pollution of the lake and the shore, the breakdown of the grossly overloaded septic system and the poor state of the huts because of overcrowding, all spelt its doom.

In 1952 Kunama Lodge was added to the chain, but after only four years a rare avalanche, rushing down the 270 metre high, steep-sided valley, swept most of it away, killing a girl trapped inside. The third chalet, Illawong, is the only one of the three that has survived, though it too has not been used as a chalet for years. An extension of a much older hut, Pounds Creek, it has probably been used by more old timers than any other hut in the mountains.

Overcrowding in the huts, especially those near the entrances to the snowfields, is undeniably a problem and has sometimes resulted in sanitation problems and sickness. But the weather in the mountains can swing treacherously from one mood to another. Out of a blue sky can come driving rain, sleeting horizontally across the ground, followed by freezing blizzards that can white out the whole range in minutes, even at the height of summer.

When this happens, even experienced skiers need to seek refuge. The Main Range poses a special danger because it is very easy to reach from the ski resorts in good weather, and extremely difficult to get out of when the weather turns.

Banjo Paterson's High Country

Two huts in the Kiandra region—
Four Mile Hut (above) *and Broken Dam*
(opposite).

Even on the easy, undulating country around Kiandra, which is so appealing to inexperienced skiers, as well as being the starting point for many cross-country tours and walks, there are dangers. It is heavily wooded in places and navigating woods is always tricky, especially on overcast days: when a dense fog blankets the area and strange magnetic anomalies play havoc with a compass, the risk increases alarmingly. Knowing that there is a hut where one can take refuge can mean the difference between life and death.

People will always find themselves in the wrong place at the wrong moment, and in the high country, the simplest accident which can overtake anyone without warning— broken equipment, injury and illness, a flooded river—can turn into a disaster. Aesthetically incongruous some of the huts may be—though even the crudest of them, with their corrugated walls and wobbly roofs, can look positively enchanting mantled in snow, or half hidden amongst the trees—but they do what the huts were always intended to do, they save people's lives.

There are a few features of the huts which are not so endearing, unless one has a curious taste in pets. Bush rats, like humans, are attracted by the warmth of the huts and the prospect of a meal. All food has to be stored in rat-proof tins, and tall stories abound of skiers waking to find squeaking rats trying to drag them across the floor by their hands.

Klaus Hueneke, in *Kiandra to Kosciusko*, describes a night when he was staying at Bradley's Hut, near Round Mountain, that must come close to many people's worst nightmare. It was bitterly cold and he drifted off to sleep dreaming of warm fur next to his cold nose and around his head.

"It suddenly dawned on me that rats were playing slippery-dips on my sleeping bag and frolicking in my hair. A gentle dream suddenly became an awesome, frightful, living nightmare. I quickly clenched my eyes tight, rolled, cavorted and snorted until they had been frightened into the farthest corners of their fireplace burrows and I, after some controlled heavy breathing, went back to sleep." General anaesthesia would not persuade most people back to sleep after that experience.

Coolamine: a mountain outpost

The century old buildings at Coolamine have enjoyed the most elaborate restoration of all the high country huts, although to describe Coolamine as a "hut" is a little incongruous. Its two homesteads and rambling outbuildings give it more the appearance of a substantial country home, which indeed is what it once was.

Coolamine is at the top end of the Kosciusko Park, between the Fiery Range and the Brindabellas, about 30 kilometres north-east of Kiandra. It was originally an outstation of Yarralumla, the selection of the Irish-born pastoralist and politician, Sir Terence Murray, which eventually became the Governor-General's official residence. In 1891, that other remarkable pastoral family, the Campbells, who lived next door to Murray at Duntroon, acquired Yarralumla and with it its outstations which included Coolamine. The Campbells shared Murray's interest in Coolamine and sent their own overseer, George Southwell to replace Murray's overseer, Stewart Maule.

Southwell arrived with a bullock team and a young wife riding side-saddle beside him, clutching their baby. He lost no time building a house for them, constructing it from wooden slabs which he shaped and joined so that each slab slightly overlapped the one below, to produce a weatherboard effect that prevented water from seeping through the cracks. The inside of the walls was lined with newspapers for insulation, and a brick and mortar chimney carried away the smoke from the fire.

In the years that followed, Coolamine grew. A second homestead was built—so that Campbell and his family could spend a part of each summer there—an interesting house, with an unusually high-pitched roof and a very tall chimney. They added a post office and a log cheese-house; vegetable gardens and an orchard were planted; and a race line brought water to the property from a creek behind a nearby hill.

Like all properties of the time, Coolamine had to be as self-sufficient as possible. Apart from the odd travelling salesman who called, such as the Sikh who came every year selling dresses and materials, stores came in only twice a year, by bullock train from Queanbeyan.

The Campbells and Southwells were hospitable people and Coolamine became known for the warmth of the welcome that visitors received there. Over the years, though, the property changed hands several times and it gradually ran down. One of the last occupants resolved the problem of where to garage his battered Land Rover each winter by cutting a hole in the side of the historic old cheese-house.

By 1975, when the last of the freehold enclaves were absorbed into the park, Coolamine had

(opposite) *Coolamine before restoration.*

(above) *Wheel of derelict cart at Coolamine.*

Coolamine: a mountain outpost

degenerated into such a state that it seemed doomed to end its long and colourful life as a heap of rubble in the valley. It was little more than a skeleton when the National Parks and Wildlife Service and the Australian Heritage Commission made the enlightened decision that Coolamine deserved better and would be fully restored.

Many of the slabs had been burnt, the floorboards eaten by wildlife and most of the iron prised from the roof and taken away. A team of volunteers was recruited, many of whom had little knowledge of bushcraft, but under the guidance of a capable bush craftsman, they learned new skills in working with wood, using traditional techniques. They learned to use a broad axe, to produce slabs with a few deft blows and to draw a straight line on wood by the centuries old method of dipping a string in charcoal and then drawing it tight and flicking it on to the logs.

Floors were relaid with rough-sawn timber and new slabs replaced those which had disappeared. A two-seater dunny was affectionately brought back to life. Only similar materials to those that had been used in the original buildings were permitted and a truck-load of Alpine ash was purchased.

The result is the equal of anything that its original builders could have aspired to.

Water race to dam at Coolamine (opposite).

(left) *Coolamine homestead.*

Kosciusko National Park

It is strange that the Kosciusko National Park, conceived with so many good intentions, should so often become embroiled in bitter controversy; yet this seems to be the fate of national parks the world over. The difficulty, of course, is that people look to their parks to fulfil so many needs—in the Kosciusko Park, the resort developers need their tourists, the skiers want to ski, the naturalists ask only to be left alone and the more extreme environmentalists hanker for the park to revert to its natural inhabitants and for all development and most humans to be excluded.

The Sisyphean task of the rangers is to try to achieve the impossible goal of satisfying all these usually conflicting demands; inevitably, they run the risk of pleasing nobody.

Proclaimed in 1940, the Kosciusko National Park incorporates some of the loveliest and most unspoilt areas of the high country. Stretching over 650,000 hectares, it extends north from the Victorian border, across the Snowy Mountains and right up to the Brindabellas outside Canberra. Conservationists have a dream of a contiguous national park, extending from the outskirts of Canberra to within sight of Melbourne, and it is already well advanced.

The park includes ten mountain peaks above 2100 metres and some of the rarest plants and most ecologically fragile land in Australia. Unspoilt Aboriginal cave paintings are carefully protected and a large part of the park has now been declared a wilderness, effectively preventing any interference in that area at all.

Yet at the same time, it has to accommodate within its borders one of the largest hydro-electric schemes in the world, a major winter ski industry, built at a time when environmental safeguards were the last thing on anybody's mind and 1600 kilometres of roads and tracks. Policing the park, with this network of roads and a staff stretched to its limits, is a nightmare; park staff can hardly control the well-intentioned visitors from trampling over fragile country. Bird and reptile smugglers often are able to operate unscathed.

Any park manager would be taxed to cope with an increasing migration of tourists into their park each year. But in addition to this they must also cope with great stretches of aerial power lines, whose broad easement must be kept chemically cleared of trees and shrubs; and the superstructure associated with the hydro-electric scheme. These dams, power stations, tunnel and aqueduct systems and their pumping stations all require constant supervision to ensure that their existence does not pose a threat to the environment of the national park. The wonder is that the park is still so unspoilt, so utterly peaceful away from the frenzied crowds on the ski slopes.

The Kosciusko National Park encompasses some of the loveliest areas of the high country. From a tapestry of wildflowers in summer, the country is transformed into a wonderland of grey and white in winter.

(top) The fox leaves a distinctive track in the fresh snow, while the wombat (above) leaves a pigeon-toed track on his trips to forage for roots and sedge-like plants.

91

Kosciusko National Park

Proclaimed in 1940, Kosciusko National Park incorporates 650,000 hectares of high country. Wildflowers blanket the slopes in summer and the melting snow gives rise to sparkling clear waterfalls. Huts such as Pretty Plain provide shelter for bushwalkers caught in the unpredictable weather of the mountains.
(below) *Kosciusko National Park Rangers on patrol in the Byadbo wilderness area.*

be an intrinsic part of the park's ecology after so many generations, can cause a great deal of damage with their hooves. But this damage is nothing compared with that caused by the wild pigs.

Pigs are formidable survivors. You can shoot one or two or a hundred, but unless you decrease the population of an area by at least 80 per cent, culling will have almost no impact. Research into the pig's breeding habits and distribution is a high priority (considering their visibility and size, surprisingly little is known about their breeding habits) for without this knowledge, no real control work is possible. It is very important because the pig is a most destructive, and sometimes a very dangerous, animal.

Dogs are not such a problem, except for the graziers whose country abuts the park, although packs of as many as 20 dogs have been sighted. Most are not full-blood dingoes, but domestic and working dogs that are either left free to wander at night, or have gone wild.

So far as the ecology of the park is concerned, cats are a more serious problem. Semi-wild domestic cats proliferated at the 120-odd camps and townships used during the construction of the hydro-electric scheme, and when these settlements closed down, many of the cats were left behind and allowed to run wild.

To the casual observer, the high country can seem devoid of life. There are none of the great animal populations of the African plains and foothills, just the occasional hare, conspicuous against the snow, or a fox trotting purposefully past as he goes about his nefarious business.

Many of the creatures are nocturnal and some actually spend much of the winter under the snow. The rare Mountain Pygmy possum lives like this. When it was systematically studied the only way that the researcher could keep in touch with it was with a radio transmitter. The little possum is so specialised that it is found only in the alpine and subalpine areas of the Kosciusko Park and across the border on the Hotham-Bogong high plains.

Another curious little animal that is rarely seen unless one specifically looks for it, is a little marsupial mouse called an antechine. The most remarkable thing about the antechine is its extraordinary sex life. Not only is it extremely energetic and noisy for its size, but it can keep up its frantic love-making for up to 12 hours. When it's over, both mice

In summer the ranges are carpeted with flowers that leave the soft morning air heady with their perfume; in winter, the park is breathtaking with its spectacular scenery and frightening for the unpredictability of its treacherous weather.

For more than 130 years, before there was any thought of creating a park in this country, the area encompassed by the national park was used for summer grazing. The arguments for and against grazing are complex, but the trauma that many families suffered when they were thrown off this land after generations of caring for the hills as well as taking from them, has never been entirely overcome.

Animals that are unwelcome in the park are a constant worry. Even the brumbies, which can reasonably claim to

94

emerge battered and bloodied and the male is so exhausted that he not infrequently dies after a single breeding season. The female appears to be made of sterner stuff because she can survive for as many as three seasons before the sheer effort of it all proves too much.

The rats in the mountains are mostly bush rats, but there is a rare creature called the broad-toothed rat, which was apparently a survivor of the last Ice Age. Its image suffers from being labelled a rat, but in fact it is an entirely innocuous creature.

The bird life is surprisingly sparse. Hawks and eagles are never far away, the wedge-tail soaring effortlessly over its mountain domain, still maligned and shot indiscriminately by some for imagined wrongs. The black cockatoos shriek their warning as they hurl themselves through the teeth of a storm and the soft pink and grey of the gang gangs is a friendly and welcome sight. Diminutive brown pipits flitter between tussocks and shrubs, always close to the ground; and higher up, the ravens congregate raucously when the bogong moths provide them with their summer feast.

The sphagnum bogs are home to an array of croaking, grunting, booming frogs, among them the wasp-coloured black and yellow Corroboree frog, only 2.5 centimetres long but perhaps the most familiar of all Australian frogs. There are lovely butterflies and moths, perhaps none more so than the beautiful Alpine Swallowtail.

The aim of the park managers is to make some part of the park available for all the different demands being made on it, but no park can be available in its entirety to everyone. Buses used to snarl up the hill to the summit of Kosciusko, polluting the clean mountain air with their noise and the stench of their fumes. When commonsense prevailed and the buses were stopped, there was an angry outburst from a few people who insisted that, as part owners of the park, they were entitled to drive anywhere within it. Obviously, though, the major issue for a National Park is the preservation of the environment, and no park could accept this idea.

It is hoped, instead, that the people of Australia will be able to appreciate, and have the use of, a magnificent national park which attempts to satisfy most of its visitors most of the time.

(opposite) *Emus are rather an unusual sight in the Snowy Mountains, far from their usual dryland habitat. There are large numbers in the mountains, however, particularly in the Cabramurra, World's End and lower Snowy River areas. They seem to exist quite adequately by foraging on vegetables and grubs.*

The rare mountain pygmy possum (top) *was thought to be extinct until 1966, when they were found in the heath-covered boulder slopes of the sub-alpine and alpine areas of the Kosciusko National Park. The corroboree frog* (centre) *lives in sphagnum moss beside creeks and bogs in a sub-alpine area during summer and hibernates in winter. Echidnas are frequently seen in wooded areas* (bottom).

An era ends: Tom and Mollie Taylor

There are many good reasons for including the old homestead complex of Currango, near Lake Tantangara, in any book about the high country, and none better than Tom and Mollie Taylor, the last of the old mountain pioneers to be allowed to keep their home in the park. When they closed the door of the old homestead behind them, their home for more than 40 years, it was a very sad moment for this endearing couple; but for the high country it was the end of a way of life, the closing of a chapter that had begun more than 150 years before.

Tom came to the mountains when he was four, when his father, William, took over the management of Coolamine from Campbell's first overseer, George Southwell. William stayed for 30 years. Mollie's parents, meanwhile, were living on the blacksoil plains of Narromine, north-west of Sydney. Both Mollie and Tom grew up with an abiding love and understanding of the bush.

When she was only 17, Mollie was already working as a governess on a remote property. She then moved to Sydney, where she found employment at the Arnotts biscuit factory. This stint at the biscuit factory made Mollie determined that she was never again going to live in the city. She took up bushwalking because it gave her an excuse to get out of the city; and it was on a trip to the Yarrangobilly Caves that she met Tom, who had ridden in from Coolamine to the Rules Point Hotel where she was staying. They married in 1935.

Tom took Mollie home to Coolamine, where she lost no time making a few changes—she ripped up the floor of the main room to start with, because it was sagging alarmingly in the middle; and they papered all the walls with real wallpaper—"I couldn't stand newspaper".

They arrived when the horse and buggy were still far more visible on the country roads than motor cars. "If I had a letter to post," Mollie recalls, "I saddled up a horse and went to Rules Point to post it. There was no moaning and groaning then about having to travel 12 miles to post a letter!"

She was an excellent horsewoman and maintains that the only time she lost her independence was when the saddle came off her horse—"I never did learn to drive a vehicle".

To listen to Mollie, every day spent in the bush was idyllic. "I wouldn't have cared where it was, as long as I was in the bush," she says with conviction, but times must have been very hard some years. Within a few years of being married, they were living in Pocket's Hut, a remote place about ten kilometres from Coolamine; and then Spencer's Hut, while Tom did a bit of gold-mining, stock work and anything else he could put his hand to. Mollie dismisses the idea

(opposite) *Tom Taylor, raconteur and mountain philosopher; and Currango, the Taylors' home until they moved to Tumut in 1988.*

 *Tom and Mollie Taylor epitomise the mountain tradition of hospitality and friendship, photographed here on the day of their departure from their much loved mountain home, Currango; a collection of homestead, men's quarters and old sheds.*

 (opposite) *The old Currango homestead.*

that because they were hard up, their lives were in any way impoverished. "As long as you're with somebody that you love and you want to spend your life with, what does it matter whether you're rich or poor?" is her reply.

Then in 1944, the Kosciusko Park was proclaimed and the government began the long business—it took them 20 years—of removing the stock.

They began on the Main Range, then moved on to Jagungal and finally cleared the northern plains. Tom became a ranger with the Lands Department, which controlled the high country during the stocking period. His job was to make sure that no one was over-grazing the country where they were still allowed to have stock, by taking in more than they were permitted; and that they stayed away from the areas that were now banned to all stock.

Tom carried out his duties with the Lands Department with tact. Although his job, in everything but name, was a Lands Department policeman, enforcing a law that was bitterly resented by the graziers, you never hear a bad word said about the way he carried it out. He still believes that it was a grave mistake to keep sheep out of the whole of the park, when there was no alternative method for keeping the weeds down and reducing the fire risk.

That same year, Currango, 20 kilometres from Coolamine, was resumed by the park which offered it to Tom and Mollie

with security of tenure for the rest of their lives. It is a sprawling collection of homestead, outhouses and shearers' quarters on the eastern side of the valley of Tantangara dam, which dams the Murrumbidgee. The name Currango is a corruption of Gurrangorambla, the range of hills behind the property.

Enormous pine trees shield the homestead against the weather, and two old cottages, Daffodil and The Pines, with no electricity and charming old furniture, have given great joy to friends and fishermen who have sampled the Taylor's well known hospitality over the years.

When they drove away from Currango for the last time, Mollie was 86, Tom a couple of years younger, though they both seem younger. Tom is a philosopher, in constant search of the ultimate meaning of things. He is also an inexhaustible raconteur, who has been known to climb from a sick bed at four in the afternoon and still be telling tales seven hours later, with barely a question allowed to interrupt the flow!

They left knowing that there was every likelihood that Currango would be restored and preserved, though for what, nobody seemed sure. For Mollie it was enough that it was going to be saved. "I have been very lucky that I could spend so many years in this beautiful place," she reflected. "None of that need change when we have gone."

An era ends: Tom and Mollie Taylor

Harnessing the Snowy

Australia is the driest continent on earth, save for the Antarctic, and water is its most precious resource. So it was no wonder that almost from the time when the Snowy Mountains were discovered, men should have turned their imaginations to devising some way of harnessing the waters of the Snowy River, which received much of the enormous precipitation of snow and rain that fell on the mountains. The challenge was to divert the Snowy's waters, which ran south through country that had no need of irrigation, straight into the Bass Strait; and use it instead to irrigate the frequently drought-stricken plains on the other side of the Great Divide.

Initial planning of the Scheme began before the war ended and work started in 1949. It lasted for 25 years. The aim was not only to provide electricity to meet peak demand in both Victoria and New South Wales (a hydro-electric supply can be brought into service and closed down very rapidly to meet sudden surges in demand), but the diverted water would irrigate great areas of previously dry land on the western side of the mountains.

It involved damming the turbulent Snowy River and its main tributary, the Eucumbene, on the eastern side of the Great Divide; and then, through a series of tunnels bored under the mountains, diverting the water into the two great river systems, the Murray and the Murrumbidgee on the western side of the mountains, to irrigate the dry plains.

In effect, the Snowy Mountains became an enormous power station, with 16 dams (the largest, Lake Eucumbene, has nine times the volume of water of Sydney Harbour), seven power stations, 80 kilometres of aqueduct and 145 kilometres of tunnel. The fall of 915 metres, as the water flows through the tunnels and shafts under the mountains, is used to generate electricity in the seven power stations, four of them in the rugged Tumut Gorge. So totally has the water been brought under control, that it can be reversed and pumped back uphill again from the Tumut to Lake Eucumbene, if the flow downstream or the level of the lake requires it.

Men and women from 27 nations worked on the Snowy scheme and 121 died there. Many lived in new townships and settlements that sprang up around the mountains, and in remote camps, working for much of the year in appalling conditions. For 109 days each year on average they had to contend with storms and blizzards, gale-force winds, heavy snowfalls and sub-zero temperatures.

Some of the best hydro-electric engineers and dam builders in the world were assembled in Cooma, the headquarters of the Snowy Mountains Hydro-electric Authority. Many remained behind when the project was completed to form the international consultancy, the Snowy Mountains Engineering Corporation.

(opposite) *The Talbingo–Tumut Dam is one of 16 built during the Snowy Scheme era.*

The Jindabyne valley as many old–timers would remember it (top), *and as it is today* (above).

Miles Franklin's Tumut Valley

Tumut, with its shady, tree-lined avenues and perfect setting of river and mountains, is that real rarity in rural Australia—a very attractive country town. The first village there, named Mill Angle, grew up around a bridge that was built over the dangerous Tumut River in 1847. Even by present day standards, the toll exacted was exorbitant, with pedestrians and horses forced to pay a shilling, and drays and wagons a pound. Those who couldn't afford the toll used a punt or forded the river when it was low, but in winter and spring, when the Tumut was in spate, they either found another crossing place, or they didn't go over the river.

In 1852, there was a great flood that swept the village away and drowned 50 people, and the present town, on a safer site, dates from then. The Kiandra gold rush gave Tumut a useful boost (1200 men were reported to have passed through the town in four days in 1860); and when the rush was over and the fields had been worked out many of the same miners and prospectors, including a number of Chinese who grew vegetables and tobacco on the river flats, settled there.

The Tumut River is perhaps the most beautiful of all the mountain streams. Rising high in the ranges around Jagungal, it flows through the high plain country of Happy Jacks and Doubtful River, a mecca for trout fishermen from all over the country. Beautiful in summer, but treacherous with its sudden floods and clear, icy water, it has caused many tragedies over the years, most of them when men have tried to cross it in spate, or have swum in it.

Talbingo was, many claim, the most perfect part of this perfect stream, with lovely pools and rapids to challenge fishermen when trout fishing was still an art and before spinning gear was ever thought of. Every corner and pool had its name and its devoted fishermen who returned to the same spot, year after year. From the old pub to the big bend to the east, where the power station is now, there was Pulpit Rock, the Mill Pond, Island Stretch and Gum Hole Tree. Talbingo itself was always "The Foot".

Changing seasons in the poplar plantations at Tumut.

Times change. They have dammed the valley now and these private places are no more. When we were writing this book, a storeman with the Snowy Mountains Authority brought in a splendid trout he had taken. He had shot it . . .

The name Talbingo, like so many that sound authentic, is not truly Aboriginal, but a corruption, probably of two words, "bingo" or "binji" meaning a belly, and "tal" a derivation of the English word tall, hence "big belly". From a distance, and with a considerable stretch of the imagination, Mount Talbingo looks like the large belly of a man lying down. There were many Aboriginals here at one time, but there is no record of any bloodshed or cruelty at the hands of the Europeans.

Banjo Paterson's High Country

As the normal food supplies and the lives and ceremonials of these Aboriginals were interfered with, even without malice, they just drifted away, and by 1870, there were almost none left in this area. In 1875, the last leader of this district, Wellington, and his wife Sally, died and were buried in what is now the showground paddock.

The explorer Hamilton Hume, a great mediator, was largely responsible for this peaceful interlude with the Aboriginals. He was probably the first white man to see Talbingo when he passed through on the western side of the Tumut River, with William Hovell, in November 1824.

The present township of Talbingo is a new creation, for there was no town before the valley was flooded, only a few houses, a pub and a garage. This attractive town was built for men working on the hydro-electric scheme.

Talbingo had its share of characters who are still remembered with pleasure. There was Jimmy McNamara who couldn't write or read or count money and never went to school, but who was blessed with a touchingly simple logic. The wind blew his hut down one winter and the holes that he dug for the new door were a shade too deep. For the rest of his life, he lived in a house with a front door that was only 90 cm high. "It keeps the stock out," he explained when he felt the need to justify the door.

Then there was Skinny Hudson, a timber-getter all his life and as rough and rugged as they come. (His real name was Cyril, but he could not live with that.) A good poacher, he loved to get up early before the forestry rangers and bring in a load of purloined timber. When they caught him red-handed one day and hauled him before the court, he sent a mate to court in his place and went out and stole another load to pay for his fine.

They found a man called Sinclair dead in the camp on the Jounama Creek one morning, not far from where Talbingo township stands today. The police and a doctor came out from Tumut in a sulky and his mates wrapped him in a blanket and buried him in the side of the hill. Alfred Hitchcock was given the job of undertaker because he was the only one with a black horse, and as Jack Spring was the best talker, he had the task of reading the burial service. Towards the end, Spring strayed a little from the authorised version and finished with the words, "Sleep well, you poor bastard". The cross of stones they laid on the

hillside is still there.

For most Australians, however, Talbingo's fame centres on one person, the author Miles Franklin, who was born there and for whom the valley was always the dearest place on earth. "Quite plain, but the nicest person you could meet," she was born in 1879 in the homestead of her grandparents, Oltman and Sarah Lampe, who were pioneers in the district. Her mother had ridden over the mountains from Brindabella to have the baby at Talbingo and then rode back with the baby Miles on a pillow in front of her saddle.

It was at Talbingo, in her childhood, that the lyrebirds came down off the hill and fed with the fowl. She was able to catch them because they cannot fly uphill. And it was from Talbingo that her enormous love and understanding of the country stemmed. In the foreword to "My Brilliant Career", the book by which she will always be remembered, Henry Lawson (who thought she was a man when she first wrote to him), wrote, "Her book is true to Australia—the truest I have ever read." When Miles Franklin died in 1954, at the age of 75, she directed that her ashes be strewn in the Jounama Creek, where they would be carried down to the Tumut River. She didn't live to see her lovely valley flooded, and the homestead, which the Lampes built to replace the one where she was born after it burnt down, disappear under the water.

THE SOUTHERN CLOUD

High on a hillside at World's End, in the Toolong Range near Tooma Dam, lies the tangled, rusting remains of an old aircraft. Bushfires and the ravages of 50 years have made it almost unrecognisable. There is no hint that these are the remnants of an aviation tragedy that destroyed an airline and baffled Australians for nearly 30 years.

At 8.00 a.m. on a wet Sydney morning in March 1931, a three-engined Avro 10, the "Southern Cloud", took off for Melbourne and disappeared from view. More than 27 years would pass before any trace of it was seen again.

The weather that morning was appalling over the Snowy Mountains, which lay on the direct route from Sydney to Melbourne, and Captain T. W. Shortbridge would have encountered violent turbulence, heavy rain and icing even before he was over the mountains.

Weather forecasting then was a hit-and-miss affair, with pilots of early morning flights having to rely on the forecast in the newspapers, because the meteorological office was only open during office hours.

When the aircraft didn't arrive in Melbourne, a massive search began and went on for days, without finding anything. The "Southern Cloud" had vanished.

The disappearance of the plane, which was owned by Charles Kingsford-Smith and Charles Ulm's Australian National Airways, became a cause celèbre. Kingsford-Smith and Ulm were desperate to secure the government mail subsidy between the two cities, without which their struggling airline had no chance of survival. Their implacable rival was an unglamorous little airline called the Queensland and Northern Territory Aerial Service—Qantas—and its ultra-cautious founder, Hudson Fysh.

Fysh made no secret of his contempt for the A.N.A. philosophy that the mail must get through at any cost and he was convinced that recklessness caused the loss of the "Southern Cloud". Fairly or not, the stories of A.N.A. pilots flying by the seat of their pants were soon circulating, and public confidence in the airline evaporated. It went out of business, leaving Hudson Fysh to pick up the subsidy. Had it not been for the "Southern Cloud" tragedy it is arguable that A.N.A. and not Qantas would have become the national airline.

Not a single clue to the whereabouts of the missing plane was found until 27 years later, Tom Sonter, a young Snowy Mountains Hydro-electric Authority worker was walking in the Toolong Range, 15 kilometres north-west of Jagungal. He climbed up through the undergrowth on a steep hillside rising sharply from the valley, turned to take a photograph and stepped back onto a rusty piece of tubular steel. The "Southern Cloud" had finally been found.

The plane had flown into the hill 80 metres below the summit. It had been steeply banked to the right at the moment of impact, perhaps because Shortbridge had seen too late that he was flying into the mountain. It was in any event 25 kilometres off course. Whether Shortbridge had decided to risk the weather and fly over the mountains, or was pushed far to the east by the storm in spite of trying to fly around it by diverting over Goulburn.

Today, a few pieces of the Avro, salvaged from the wreckage, sit rather forlornly in a concrete cage beside the main road out of Cooma, a sun-bleached RAAF flag hanging beside them. At the site of the crash, which is almost inaccessible, there is an incongruous monument, adorned with pink ceramic flowers. Both seem inadequate memorials to one of the great aviation mysteries of our time.

 *Southern Cloud wreckage.*

The high plains of Victoria

For a state that takes up only three per cent of the Australian continent, Victoria has a remarkably varied geology, with harsh desert in the west, snow-capped mountains in the north-east, and, to north and south, some of the most fertile country in Australia.

Most of Victoria's high country is a continuation of the Great Dividing Range that sweeps down from the Snowy Mountains. The highlands at the border are about 300 kilometres in width, but they gradually become lower and narrower as they arc westward across the state for 650 kilometres, before ending in the Grampians and the Dundas Highlands, less than 50 kilometres from the South Australian border.

The highlands are briefly broken by the Kilmore Gap, north of Melbourne, where the main road and railway to the north converge to cross the Dividing Range. When they resume on the western side of the gap, they are much gentler, the hills seldom rising above 900 metres and the ranges often separated by broad expanses of quite softly undulating country.

The eastern highlands on the other side of the gap, however, are far different. They become steeper and more unfriendly the further east they go. Though not as high as the highest mountains in the Main Range (Kosciusko is 242 metres higher than Mount Bogong, Victoria's tallest mountain), and without the immense open areas on top of the Snowy Mountains, the Victorian Alps, with their steep, inaccessible spurs and ridges, their densely wooded sides, and dark, narrow valleys gouged deeply into the hills by perennial streams, are even more impenetrable and inhospitable. It is no surprise that parts of this wild country have scarcely been explored.

Below about 1250 metres, the slopes of the hills and mountains and the ridges and spurs are heavily timbered with mountain ash and woollybutts, but above that, the snow gums take over, the only trees that can survive the bleak winter conditions at this altitude. The tree-line ends altogether at about 1850 metres and beyond that there is only windswept grass and the hardiest herbs that thrive in these sub-zero temperatures, often buried under a deep layer of snow. Above 1600 metres snow lies for up to five months of the year, on country where flowers bloom in profusion through spring and summer.

The rivers on the northern side of the watershed run into the Murray and four of them, the Mitta Mitta, Ovens and Kiewa, and the King further to the west, flow through wide fertile valleys. But on the southern side, numerous permanent creeks are contained in narrow valleys and become fast and dangerous torrents when they are fed by melting snow and rain. They eventually run into Bass Strait.

The Fitzgerald family take their cattle up to their Mount Nelse lease on the Bogong High Plains each summer. (above) *Early morning in the mountains.*

The high plains of Victoria

The steep slopes and long, hard winters discourage almost any attempt at agriculture, apart from a few hop and tobacco farms in the most sheltered valleys. But high in the hills, often hidden from view until one is almost upon them, are plateaux and rolling plains which provide rich grazing. Some of Australia's finest beef cattle are raised here. The plains vary in size from great tracts of land extending over tens of thousands of hectares, to mere pockets of grassland high on the ridges between the valleys.

For 18 years after Mark Currie first gazed across the open plains of the Monaro, this land beyond the mountains to the south remained a part of New South Wales. Not until 1851 was Victoria proclaimed a separate colony.

While development went on spasmodically around Port Phillip Bay, squatters on the Monaro were preoccupied with finding new pastures, particularly as they were enduring a disastrous drought through much of the 1830s. This unknown, uncharted land on the other side of the mountains taxed their imaginations constantly. The main barrier that confronted them was not the intransigence of the government in Sydney, which they were quite prepared to ignore, but the forbidding nature of the country itself.

A shadowy figure in history, Edmund Buckley, appears to have been the first European to venture far into the remote hills and valleys of north-eastern Victoria. He seemed to have travelled entirely alone and without stock, yet he went as far south as Ensay, on the other side of the eastern highlands.

James Macfarlane, who would prove himself to be a very canny Scot, already had a run high in the Berrima Range that was just—by less than two kilometres—on the Victorian side of the line that became the border between the two colonies; but it was a squatter named Charles Ebden who is credited with being the first man to deliberately drive cattle into north-eastern Victoria.

A wealthy man when he came to Australia from South Africa (and he became a great deal wealthier), Ebden had suffered a severe fire on his cattle run at Tarcutta, near Wagga Wagga, and in October 1835, he sent his stockman, William Wyse, across the Murray in search of new pastures.

Wyse established a run, which he called Mungabareena, near what would become a major crossing over the Murray, the town of Albury, and some weeks later, a second run

The Barry Way is today's link between the Monaro and the high plains of Victoria. The Moonbah cemetery, on the Jindabyne end of the Barry Way contains the graves of early pioneers who first ventured south over the border, past Ingebyra and the Pinch River.

(above) The Snowy River is the source of much of Australia's folklore and history.

(opposite) Lisa Caldwell is one of a new generation of women who take to the mountains with the same spirit as the early pioneers.

this hazardous descent to the valley floor has been known as Jacob's Ladder.

They would have been well down the spur before they caught their first glimpse of the Snowy River through the trees, swift-flowing at all times and when in spate from the snow melt or heavy rains, dangerous and turbulent.

Once in the valley, they splashed through Jacob's River, which runs into the Snowy at the foot of the Ladder, and keeping to the Snowy's west bank, travelled on towards the south. Sometimes the going was easy, sometimes they were forced up on to the sides of hills so steep that they threatened to overturn the drays. The men removed the top-side wheels and replaced them with iron-rimmed hubs to try to keep the drays on an even keel. For every stockman who followed, an iron nave, or hub, became an obligatory piece of equipment.

For ten kilometres they followed the Snowy, then came to a place where a sizeable creek came in on their right leading up into the hills from the valley. Just after this, they found their way blocked by a steep hill and the river turned sharply to the west. They were faced with the choice of either following it in this new direction, or of going back to the creek and leaving the valley. In fact, the Snowy only followed the base of the hill and resumed its southerly journey on the other side. Others coming after them would continue down the river into the remote valley of Suggan Buggan and then on to the fertile plains of Gippsland, but McKillop and Livingstone chose to go back to the creek, later named Pinch River.

The next 15 or so kilometres are exhausting when one's only load is a light pack. Burdened as they were, one can only marvel at their fortitude as they climbed beside the Pinch River for three kilometres, then went up very steeply for 1000 metres. Once up that rise, they would have struggled laboriously up one steep, narrow spur after another, somehow coaxing and bullying the bullocks and horses on to slopes that look impossible, finally coming out on the tops of the Suggan Buggan Range.

As they climbed, they left behind the pine-covered spurs and moved into snow gum country. The bellbirds' calls still followed them, but the raucous ravens now clamoured loudest to be heard.

This long wearisome haul out of the Snowy River valley

at the junction of the Kiewa and the Murray a few kilometres to the south-west.

Meanwhile, another party, further to the east on the Monaro, was preparing to set out on a journey of exploration into the mountains that was to prove much more difficult and hazardous. George McKillop and George Livingstone were both settlers and their aim was to establish a stock route between the Monaro and Port Phillip Bay.

With bullock wagons to carry their supplies, but no maps to guide them, they travelled down through Moonbah and Ingebyra, past the place where the ruins of the old Moonbah homestead still stand forlornly on a hill above the small, willow-lined lake that provided its water.

Their route followed closely the modern Barry Way, a winding, dusty back-road into Victoria. It comes suddenly to the edge of a steep, pine-timbered ridge high above the Snowy River valley, and the little party would have made its way cautiously down the precipitous spur, their horses and bullocks slithering on the slippery pine needles that lay across their track. Since the earliest pioneering days, has always been known, with no affection at all, as the Nine Mile. One of the Pendergasts once carried water in a horse rug to the very top of the Nine Mile to men who were knocked up taking a mob of cattle up the hill.

The journey was still far from over, even now. They crossed the Suggan Buggans, dropped down to the Ingeegoodbee River, went up again on to the Berrima Range and found themselves on James Macfarlane's remote run, east of the Pilot, a 1750 metre mountain that rises high above the surrounding country. (Macfarlane had come down through Tin Mines and along the Ingeegoodbee, not over Jacob's Ladder.) It is in the shadow of the Pilot that the greatest of all Australia's rivers, the Murray, begins its life as the Indi, a small, happy stream, that can be crossed with a single step.

The Tin Mines, to the north of the Pilot, were worked on and off for the best part of a century, but when McKillop and Livingstone passed on the south side of the mountain the discovery of tin was still 16 years away. Even the brumbies, which later bred in huge numbers in the area around the Tin Mines and were rounded up in great mobs by the brumby catchers, had not yet arrived.

At Macfarlane's Flat, as he called his run, James Macfarlane agreed to go on with them, though as events would prove, he was probably more interested in adding to his grazing runs nearer home than in forcing his way right through to the southern ocean. They dropped down to cross the Berrima Creek and immediately had to climb steeply over a spur; then down to yet another creek and up another seemingly interminable slope, fourteen and a half kilometres in length once more, and steep for every metre of the way. To see the cruel nature of this country which they slogged across makes it even more astonishing that it would become one of the most important stock routes in the south-east.

Whatever they expected at the top, it surely wasn't the sight that greeted them. For as they rounded the 1800 metre Cobberas, they emerged on to a lovely plateau almost hidden by stands of snow gum. More a chain of meadows than an unbroken plain, the Playground as it came to be called, would become an important link along the stock route, an oasis for the exhausted stockmen and their animals.

They would have rested briefly here before starting a

gradual descent, over Native Dog Creek, then Native Cat, up a short climb to the Limestone and on through Meringo and Leinster to Benambra and, finally, out on to the plains which made all the hardships of their journey bearable. They named the plains Strathdownie, which was soon replaced by the name of Macfarlane's first run there, Omeo (at first spelt Omio, supposedly Macfarlane's first reaction when he saw the plains!) For those men, and especially for McKillop and Livingstone from the drought-ravaged Monaro, these fertile plains, reaching away towards the western slopes of the Great Divide, opened the promise of a new chapter in their lives,

Life on the high plains

McKillop, Livingstone and Macfarlane spent some time exploring the plain and then Macfarlane went home, leaving McKillop and Livingstone to continue south in search of a route to Port Phillip Bay. The rewards, if they succeeded, would be enormous—direct overland access to Van Diemen's Land for the Monaro's wool and meat, and to the whole of the Port Phillip District, the major settlement in what would become Victoria. Their plan was to establish runs along the new stock route, with reliable grazing that would ensure their stock reached Port Phillip Bay in prime condition.

In fact, they made little further progress, for they found their way completely blocked by impenetrable scrub that seemed to stretch across the landscape for miles. They too went home to the Monaro. Later, in 1836, McKillop did succeed in reaching Port Phillip Bay where he took up a run, while Livingstone took up a run of his own in the foothills of the Strathbogie Range. Only Macfarlane went back to establish a permanent run on the Omeo Plains.

Macfarlane had returned a year later, this time with three different settlers. His sole purpose was to take a second look at the plains and reassure himself that they were no mirage. He climbed to the top of a mountain that is still known as Macfarlane's Lookout and from the summit saw the Strathdownie Plains stretching out ahead of him into the far distance. This was no mirage!

Macfarlane said nothing to the other three about what he had seen, and instead suggested they climb another mountain, from the top of which it was impossible to see the plains. Then he feigned illness, hurried home and immediately returned with a huge mob of cattle which he turned loose on magnificent country to the east of the great lake on the plain, claiming it all as his own. Unfortunately, we are not told how the other three reacted to the news!

Macfarlane left a stockman at Omeo to guard the cattle. Perhaps his experience had taught him that the Aboriginals quickly acquired a liking for this highly accessible instant food. Over the years, he built up his mob to more than 6000 head of cattle and when he eventually sold it, another 500 were found running wild in the nearby mountains.

The speed of development in Victoria (though it remained a part of New South Wales until 1851) was extraordinary. In 1834 the first European, Edward Henty, settled there; in 1835 the first cattle were driven in from the north; yet by 1840 almost the whole of the Western District had been settled. Two advancing waves of migration, from the Monaro and the north, and from the south and Van Diemen's Land, had met along the Loddon and Avoca Rivers near Maryborough.

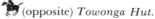 (opposite) *Towonga Hut.*

(above) *Kate Stoney.*

115

Banjo Paterson's High Country

By 1851, the land that was occupied under grazing licences was already carrying six million sheep, or two-fifths of the entire Australian flock, and beef cattle had become an important industry.

The first tentative steps on to the high plains had led to the opening up of runs in the high country all the way from Mansfield to the Cobberas and beyond. It had also been the springboard for the exploration and settlement of Gippsland and the Upper Murray and the rich, fertile valleys of the Murray's tributaries on the northern side of the watershed. For a short time, attempts were made to run sheep on the Victorian high plains, but the dingoes made it almost impossible, and unlike the New South Wales high country, it became almost exclusively cattle country.

Until 1851, the settlers on the Victorian side of the future border were controlled by the same land laws as everyone else in New South Wales, but they were even more casually enforced than on the Monaro. Few inspectors had the time or the inclination to spend days struggling down the tortuous stock route and over the ranges to Omeo and beyond to collect a dozen licence fees and count cattle.

After the new colony was established, the Victorian government was more successful than Sydney had been at curbing the squatters and at preventing them from using dummying and other tricks to secure land at the expense of the new selectors. In the land rush that followed, virtually all the country that was of any use for agriculture was taken up. The remaining marginal country in the mountains, which could only be grazed for part of the year in spite of its value in bringing stock to prime condition, was divided into extensive grazing allotments, few of them smaller than 5000 hectares.

The demand for more land was intensified by the gold fever that was sweeping Australia. Miners and prospectors rushed to every new find as it was announced and when gold was found in 1852 at Livingstone Creek in the high country (seven years before the Kiandra rush), they descended on the area in hordes. Fossicking from one end of the creek to the other, they lived in a dilapidated, filthy tent city on its banks. At first only alluvial gold was found, but soon reefs were discovered and gold mines dotted the hills and valleys.

The relics of those heady days can still be seen, the scars

and debris of an astonishing era in Australia's history. Too heavy to be packed in on horses, most of the mining equipment including the crushing plants and machinery, had been brought in by bullock train. In that unforgiving terrain the price was often high. On one journey to Omeo from Wentworth, on the Murray near Mildura, a bullocky lost twelve of his team from injuries and sheer exhaustion.

From the beginning, the high country pioneers in Victoria used bullocks and drays, typically with a team of eight or ten, although 40 or 50 and more were not unusual. There is no display of brute strength to surpass a team of bullocks under pressure, yoked together to drag a load up into the mountains. Cursed on by the bullocky, sometimes bogged down to the axles, with blows raining around them from the heavy whip handle, they went down on their knees, bellowing as they took the strain. Coming down the other side, the bullockies often tied trees to the back of the drays to act as a brake.

It was the bullocky's fearsome whip and his equally blood-curdling language that were imprinted for longest in most people's memories. The whip was up to seven metres of plaited rawhide linked to a wooden handle and always wielded with both hands. For all its length, it was an instrument of great precision. The good bullocky could flick a fly off a beast's hoof, but very rarely did he allow it to actually strike any part of the animal. Rather, with the finesse of a good fly fisherman, he would place the end of the lash delicately beside a bullock, calling at the same time. Every animal in the team had a name and it took a year to train a good bullock, longer to train the bullocky.

For many years, as in the New South Wales high country, there were no bridges and flooded mountain creeks and rivers could be impassable for weeks on end. One bullock team took 11 months to make the return journey from Omeo to Port Albert, 40 kilometres from Melbourne, in 1870.

Because of the steep terrain and the harsh winters, it was difficult to carry very large loads through the mountains with bullocks. Stockmen turned increasingly to pack horses which could carry more stores in a team, provided they weren't too bulky, and travel more easily through this country than the bullock wagons. There were usually eight or ten horses in a team and they walked loose, either following an old horse that knew the best track to take,

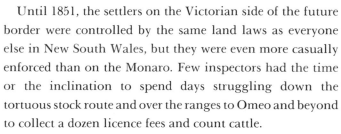

Horsemen coming up to Lovicks Hut (opposite).

(above) Young Lyric Mitchell on the Dargo High Plains.

116

or making their own way, especially between trees in wooded country.

Drays came back into favour again from Port Albert, frequently with several teams of 16 bullocks to a waggon. More than one team of 16 was needed to drag the heavy loads up some of the steep grades, over the top and down the other side.

Horse-drawn coaches were introduced later and carried passengers between Omeo and the gold mining town of Harrietville and across to Bairnsdale in Gippsland. The passengers had some unforgettable journeys. The roads were ungraded, uneven, potholed dirt tracks, usually the same ones that were used by the bullocks, and passengers, as well as holding on grimly, had to move to the top-side seats in the coach when going round the side of steep hills, in the hope that this would stop it rolling down the side.

It was going downhill, however, that the most heart-stopping moments tended to occur. Steep downhill gradients depended entirely on the coach's very basic brakes for steadying the pace, and if the brakes failed, as they not infrequently did, particularly in wet and icy weather, it meant a race to the bottom of the hill, with the horses going faster and faster, pushed on by the weight of the heavy coach, which lurched and leaped along behind them. It resembled more a Roman chariot race than public transport.

Sometimes the coach overtook the horses, like a runaway wheel on a truck. Many passengers counted themselves lucky if they and the horses and the coach all arrived at the bottom at the same time, with the coach still standing on its four wheels.

Along the stock routes there were regular camping sites and ingenuity made some of the daily chores a little easier. At most of these camping sites, for example, there was a narrow pit, about a metre deep, with a ramp at each end. The packhorses walked in at one end of this pit and could then be unloaded and re-loaded the next morning without too much lifting.

The most remarkable thing about so many of the early journeys into unexplored country is that they were made by ordinary men with no scientific training and no experience. Some were experts in their field—Thomas Mitchell was the Government surveyor, Ferdinand von Mueller and Allan Cunningham were botanists—and some,

as army and naval officers, at least had training in navigation; but most of the men who ventured into this wild, mountainous country were just farmers. What they all possessed in large measure was extraordinary courage and resourcefulness, and an obsession with finding land on which to graze their stock.

The country must have looked as daunting and dangerous as indeed it was. One slip down many of the steep-sided ridges meant certain injury or death, or the loss of vital supplies. And, although, at least initially, they had no reason to fear the Aboriginals, they were constantly looking over their shoulders, expecting to be attacked.

Pitching their tents near the tops, with an early blizzard howling over the hills, visibility down to zero and steep ravines plunging away into valleys far out of sight, must have been as hellish as it was frightening. And when the damp, heavy mists came up in the morning, blanketing the hills and filling the valleys, they must have been left with a sense of almost overpowering loneliness.

But there would also have been times, when the sky was afire with the brilliance of the stars and the moonlight fell in pools of light, the only sounds were the soft lowing of the bullocks and the shuffling of the horses, and the drawn-out howl of the dingoes that sent a shiver down the spine, when they were overawed by the unutterable beauty of it all.

Suggan Buggan

There could hardly have been a lonelier place for the early pioneers than the remote, mountain-encircled valley of Suggan Buggan, just over the border from New South Wales in the Victorian high country.

The best documented record of settlement in the valley puts two Irish-born brothers, James and Christopher O'Rourke, arriving in the valley with their families in 1838. Born in County Tipperary, they had travelled down the stock route from the Monaro, negotiating Jacob's Ladder and splashing through Jacob's River. Instead of turning right at Pinch River, however, and heading west, as McKillop and Livingstone had done, they followed the Snowy River round the hill and after climbing over the Monaro Gap, finally emerged in the valley.

But although their influence at Suggan Buggan was far greater, they were not in fact the first to settle there. We know from the O'Rourke family records that when James and Christopher arrived there, Richard Brooks, who had settled at Gegedzerick when he was only sixteen, had already opened up a run there with 500 cattle, five horses and three acres of wheat—a lot of cattle at a time when their only real value lay in boiling them down for tallow.

Presumably Brooks had travelled south in search of new grazing country, but by 1838 when the O'Rourkes turned up, he had already decided to forfeit the lease, probably because it was too remote to manage properly from Gegedzerick, even though we know that he employed a stockman there. He had called his run Waugilmoran, confusingly similar to the name that the O'Rourkes used, Wulgulmerang.

Putting togther all the pieces, we can imagine a likely scenario of what actually happened. In 1838, after an exhausting journey with their wives and children, the O'Rourke brothers arrived in the valley and found that Brooks or his man had either just moved out or were packing up to leave. Maybe they passed them, driving their big mob of cattle, as they headed back to the Monaro.

It seems that the O'Rourkes' wives found the summer climate in the valley oppressive, so they all moved up to the plateau on top of the mountains, which was 600 metres higher and much cooler. Whereas Brooks had almost certainly looked around him when he arrived and called everything he saw—mountains as well as valley—Waugilmoran, the O'Rourkes were now more specific. They called the valley itself Suggan Buggan and they named the run on which they had chosen to live, high up in the mountains, Wulgulmerang, which was as close as they could get to what they thought Brooks had used.

(opposite) *Nigel Hodge, the last living link with the O'Rourke dynasty in the Suggan Buggan area, with Norm Woodhouse on horseback.*

(above) *The first settlers to the Suggan Buggan valley travelled down the stock route from the Monaro along the Snowy River.*

Suggan Buggan

They ran this in partnership, perhaps living in the same house or close to each other, until James opened up Black Mountain run further down the range two years later, in 1840, and settled there with his family. For the next 66 years, with only occasional breaks in their ownership, the three runs, Suggan Buggan, Wulgulmerang and Black Mountain were squatted on, owned or leased by the O'Rourkes.

Others came and went between 1842 and 1858, including the ubiquitous Ben Boyd who held an extensive lease in the valley from 1842 until his spectacular crash in 1848. But after 1858, the O'Rourkes had control of the whole valley and worked closely with each other.

They kept their stock up on the plateau in spring and summer, then drove it back down to the valley before the winter snows closed in on the mountain. The track from the Suggan Buggan run to Wulgulmerang was only about 20 kilometres in length, but it was so rough and steep that it was a three hour ride on a good horse without stock.

Life must sometimes have been overbearingly hard, especially for the women. In 1851, James's four-year-old son Andrew was standing in front of the open fire when his clothes caught alight; twenty hours later he died from his burns. Both James and Christopher were away mustering, so Eliza, the child's mother, sent one of her other children on horseback to Black Mountain to tell Christopher's wife, Elizabeth, to come at once. Together, the two women dug the little boy's grave and, with their children beside them, stood round the grave and said prayers. James came back a week later and was so distressed that he sold Wulgulmerang.

Christopher O'Rourke's family knew tragedy, too. Wulgulmerang was repurchased early in 1859 by one of James's children, Christopher junior. In 1866, the elder Christopher's son, David, was living in a house on the property with his wife and a daughter, Elizabeth Ann, who was 18 months old. His wife was sick in bed and David's sister, Honoria, was looking after the children. After lunch one day David rode away without noticing that little Elizabeth Ann was following him. When the child couldn't be found, Honoria at first assumed that David had taken her for a ride, as he sometimes did, and hours passed before the alarm was sounded. A whole year would go by before her body was discovered.

(above) *A kangaroo's last line of defence when attacked by dogs is to take to the water with the aim of drowning the attacker.*

(opposite) *Sheep grazing in the Suggan Buggan valley.*

121

Banjo Paterson's High Country

David was away when a party of Aboriginals called at the house. They tried to speak to Mrs O'Rourke, but she was afraid of them and they camped by a creek for three days awaiting David's return. Only then were they able to explain that they had found Elizabeth Ann's body. She had wandered for about a kilometre and a half and had fallen over a cliff, breaking her neck. She was buried in the Black Mountain family cemetery, near her grandfather Christopher.

David was an interesting man, a tall eccentric who loved horses but seldom rode them. Because he did not care to ride and loved the bush, he travelled enormous distances on foot, carrying his rations on his back. As early as 1843 he brought 70 horses into the valley, including two good stallions from which he intended to breed, presumably for the lucrative export market to India. It was these horses that ran wild and were the forerunners to many of the brumbies in north-eastern Victoria.

Early in the new century, after 66 years in the valley and on the mountain runs above it, the O'Rourkes finally left and a new dynasty was established. In 1902, a family called Rogers came over the hills from Warrigal in Victoria and took over Black Mountain. They, too, had a hard journey with one of their children dying along the way.

Black Mountain then included only 600 acres of freehold land, but there were 400 acres of fenced leasehold country and 100,000 acres of open run. The Rogers stocked the run with drought-affected bullocks from Queensland and the profit from these allowed them to purchase Wulgulmerang in 1910. Black Mountain itself was split in two in 1933 with the second portion being renamed Rockbank.

The road through the valley continued for well over a century and became the major stock route between the Monaro, Buchan and eastern Victoria. Only when the newly formed Barry Way was opened in 1961 did the Ingeegoodbee Track, as it was always known, lost its importance and fade into mountain folklore.

There were memorable cattle drives along this route, and none is more talked about to this day more than a drive made by Henry "Bung" Harris in 1947. With only four young stockmen to help him and 23 horses, Harris brought a mob of 1000 cattle more than 2000 kilometres from Tabulam on the Queensland–New South Wales border, to

Bairnsdale in Victoria's Gippsland—without losing a single beast on the five month journey. By far the most arduous part of the drive was keeping the huge mob together along the Ingeegoodbee Track and through the Suggan Buggan valley.

The Suggan Buggan run itself eventually suffered a most ignominious fate, being carved up into almost useless 1200-acre (486 hectare) allotments for soldier-settlers, too small for them to hope to make a living. Few people live in the valley today and the little slab schoolhouse, built by James O'Rourke's son Edward so that his 13 children could receive a proper education (he hired a teacher to come to Suggan Buggan), and restored in 1972, is almost the last link with the O'Rourkes.

The odd name of Suggan Buggan has taxed many people's

This tiny slab school house with a shingle roof, built in the 1850s and restored in 1972, was where the O'Rourke children received their schooling.

122

imaginations, but it is almost certainly another link with the O'Rourkes. Coming from Tipperary, they would probably have been Gaelic-speaking, at least to the extent of using common Gaelic words. The word "sugan" in Irish means a rope made from hay or straw—the Irish peasants couldn't afford jute. Sugan was also well used for the seats of chairs which also became known as "sugans".

When the O'Rourkes journeyed to the valley for the first time, their children travelled in baskets slung across packhorses and it may well have been that they either were made in the manner of sugans or jokingly called "sugans". The most positive confirmation that this is the origin of the word is that the local pronunciation has always been "soogan", its correct Gaelic pronunciation. The Buggan part isn't a Gaelic word, but probably came about as a rhyming play on the first word, in the way that hurly-burly and hugger-mugger came into existence. Remembering how many spellings of Monaro there were, it is easy enough to accept that Sugan Bugan became Suggan Buggan.

Victoria's mountain cattlemen

If the high plains are remote and lovely places by day, at night there is a magic about them that is unsurpassed. It hardly seems possible that so many stars can fit into one sky, or shine so brightly. The hills are never quiet. All night, the white-faced heron croaks throatily till dawn, while further down, among the trees, the mournful boobook calls its gloomy cry for "more pork, more pork". When the moon is full, the spur-winged plover stays awake, adding its loud, invasive "keer-kik-ki-ki-ki" to disturb the sleep of weary stockmen, as the horses shuffle restlessly and across the valley the haunting howls of prick-eared dingoes send shivers down the spine.

They are remarkably varied, these ancient plains, some flat and lush, more like paddocks than hills; some rolling downs with rocky granite outcrops. Their peaks and creeks have splendid names, each with a story or perhaps just the product of a stockman's fertile fancy—Terrible Hollow, the Razor, the Viking and Cross-cut Saw.

The largest of them all are the Bogong high plains, 1200 square kilometres with ten peaks above 1830 metres. When cattlemen talk of the Bogong Plains, they mean not just the rolling country around Victoria's highest mountain, but the whole area of Feathertop and Hotham.

Unlike three of the other best known plains, the Bluff, Howitt and Dargo high plains, which are appendages of the Great Dividing Range, the rugged Bogong Plains are a link in the chain of the Great Divide itself. They were discovered first by Europeans when two stockmen from Cobungra Station, on the Omco Plains, were told by an Aboriginal of high plains that his people used and which they reached by following one particular spur among the maze of spurs. Cobungra eventually spread over 60,750 hectares, and included all Hotham and a substantial part of the Bogong Plains.

It has some hair-raising cattle tracks, including one down to Dargo where stockmen, cattle and horses had to walk in single file for 16 kilometres along a path 130 centimetres wide, with a sheer drop to the Dargo River 300 metres below. The cattle were split into smaller mobs and had to be kept moving: one aggressive beast turning to horn the animal behind would send both of them hurtling down to the river and certain death.

From the start, the selectors' preference was for cattle on the Victorian high plains. Cattle thrive in this country, and are not prey for dingoes. The Victorian preference for cattle farming was also curiously linked to the fact that Victoria was never a penal colony.

On the Monaro and in the Snowy Mountains extensive use was made of ticket-of-leave convicts and emancipists as shepherds and there was a large work-force of unskilled men willing to take

(opposite) Mustering party on Mount Lovick. The fire in the distance is on Mount Clear. (above) Cope Hut on the Bogong High Plains.

Victoria's mountain cattlemen

on what, almost everyone agreed, was an odious job. This labour force was not available in Victoria. Without shepherds or fences, there was no possibility of running sheep in the high country on either side of the border, because the dingoes and wild dogs killed them. One evening's carelessness by a shepherd could leave his flock decimated and, at lambing time, see every lamb destroyed.

The dingoes frightened even the shepherds. It was usually after dusk when they were most dangerous but, especially when food was short, they would attack a flock in broad daylight, sometimes in full view of the shepherd.

Early attempts by settlers to shepherd their flocks themselves on the southern plains were not successful, and they quickly turned to cattle farming. The most popular breed at that time was the shorthorn, a breed for which many cattlemen still nurse a fondness. But it soon made way for the compact red and white Hereford, probably because the Hereford endured the winters better and matured faster. The hardy Black Angus cattle have been largely ignored by the cattlemen on the high plains, although they have done well whenever they have been used.

Today, there are about 100 families with snow leases on the high plains and between them they graze some 18,000 cattle. Many can trace their occupancy back for generations and the same names recur time and again in the records. Faithfulls and Treasures, Stoneys and Lovicks, Rogers and Ryders.

The Treasures have been taking their cattle up to the Dargo high plains for well over a century and they are typical of the cattlemen, self-reliant and highly expert at their own business. The first member of this remarkable family to settle on the high plains was George Emanuel Treasure, a miner, who took the legs off two armchairs and slung them on either side of a packhorse for his two smallest children, while the next oldest rode the entire journey on the saddle in front of her mother.

So arduous was the trip that at one stage Treasure's wife begged to be left where she was, by the side of the track, even if it meant exposure to the freezing night. But he urged them on and eventually they came out on the high plains, "as level as a billiard table, with a coat of grass to cushion the feet as you walked over it".

For all its remoteness, there were already miners criss-

The Stoney family carry on a family tradition of grazing their high country lease on the Bluff and Mount Eadly Stoney area east of Mansfield.

(top) *Horses on the bluff.*
(above) *Chris, Kate and Graeme Stoney.*

Banjo Paterson's High Country

The yards scattered through the high plains of Victoria are used each summer when the cattle graze the high country. Unlike the cattle, sheep remain on the lowlands during the summer. The old shearing shed in the Ensay Valley (opposite) has been the centre of activity for decades.

crossing the Dargo Plains between the diggings, and the Treasures, who built their own house from mountain ash, 1390 metres up (it is still probably the highest homestead in Victoria), began their farming life with a few dairy cattle, selling milk, butter and cheese to the miners. Their only neighbour, five kilometres to the south, was a pub, the Halfway House, which disappeared with the last of the miners.

Many of the earliest cattlemen to use the high plains for transhumant grazing (moving stock from lowland to highland and back with the change of seasons), were miners, like George Treasure, who ran their small herds, sometimes of only 50 cattle, as a sideline. They drove them up to the plains in spring when the feed is lush, and left them there while they went back to the diggings.

The high country pasture brought the cattle to prime condition, and they proved much less susceptible to the common diseases suffered by cattle kept constantly at lower altitudes. It also meant that the lower paddocks could be rested and hay grown there for winter feed. As long as the cattle were mustered and taken out before the first winter

128

snow in about mid-April, they could fend well for themselves.

When the gold petered out, a few miners, like George Treasure, remained and became skilled cattlemen. Most, however, drifted away and the professional cattlemen took over the runs. The majority had properties on the lower slopes, or at the heads of the valleys, and as they do today, used the steep, rugged spurs as a staircase up to the plains.

Many other traditions of the early settlers are still maintained. The annual muster on the plains has become a ritual. The cattlemen scorn the modern trappings of mustering, with helicopters and trail bikes. They still do the job on horseback and up in the beautiful, lonely hills, men and women still work in exactly the same way as their forebears who helped to create the state of Victoria nearly a century and a half ago. With only their dogs to help them, they drive the cattle down to the winter grazing.

Traditionally, many of the cattlemen began to muster in the week before Easter, but occasionally, and especially in years past when the snow was much heavier than it is today, they left it too late and disaster swiftly followed. One year, an early snowfall trapped horses and cattle in 150 centimetres of soft snow. Stockmen tried to clear a path, but the mob refused to be driven and floundered into even greater danger. Three thousand of them perished.

Co-operation between families and neighbours is an indispensable part of the life of the high country cattlemen. In 1960, 600 cattle were stuck belly-deep in snow on the Bluff and King Billy leases, even though it was still only autumn. Cattlemen from all over the high country rode to the rescue, oblivious of the blizzard howling across the tops. They used everything from billy-cans to their gloved hands to dig a track that the cattle could follow for kilometres through the drifts. They had just finished the track when another blizzard wiped it out.

Exhausted as they were, they began all over again, and with time against them if the cattle were to survive, put in a new track straight down a steep and dangerous spur. This time they were luckier and managed to drive the reluctant cattle down to safety. More than 50 died, but the rest were saved.

On the small plains, where the grazing rights are often held by one family, the stockmen round up the cattle into a holding yard each day, and then, without drafting, take the whole mob down to the winter pastures. On the larger plains, where several leases adjoin and there are no fences, the muster is a communal event. Once rounded up, the cattle are drafted by their brands and by the calves running with their mothers. The most complicated muster is the Bogong high plains, the largest of all the plains, where 14 leaseholders have to muster more than 4000 head of cattle and then after drafting, drive them out along seven stock routes.

They bring in the easy cattle first, and then go after the stragglers and wanderers on the spurs and down in the valleys. In timber country, the cattle arc usually out of sight and a few always manage to elude the muster. Occasionally a beast is found that has been running wild for years and it is likely to be an evil-tempered animal that can be highly disruptive in a mob.

Mustering in this kind of country doesn't require the speed of a professional jockey; what it does need is the skill of the Man from Snowy River and a horse with good endurance. For hours on end, both must be able to cope with steep rides down into the valleys, which are often strewn with fallen trees and thick with undergrowth.

Every stockman has his tricks for luring difficult cattle out into the open. In most of the high country there is a salt deficiency in the water and grass which makes cattle crave salt. Many of the stockmen carry salt which brings the cattle ambling out of the thickets and the woods. In earlier times, with the less biddable shorthorns, the stockmen used to build small yards in the valleys and leave salt beside them at night. There would usually be a beast or two waiting for them in the morning.

Above all, the stockmen rely on their dogs. They are intensely possessive of them and guard them jealously. City people sometimes complain that bushmen are cruel to their working dogs, but these dogs are not pets; they are a vital part of a working team and are treated accordingly.

Although the high plains are cattle country, the traditional Australian cattle dog, the blue heeler, is rarely used. The heeler was deliberately bred to produce the ideal cattle dog for Australian conditions from a mixture of sheepdogs, some dingo (added to make it bite hard and low and keep silent) and then some dalmation to encourage it to protect its master's gear and to like horses.

On the high plains, however, they want a dog that is a good header (which the blue usually is not), meaning that it will go to the front of a mob and confront it head-on, as well as working the rear and the sides. They need a dog that will work out of sight of its master, down in the trees and gulleys; and they want a dog that will bark to let it be known that it has found some cattle.

The cattlemen, therefore, have spurned the pure blue heeler and use instead traditional sheep dogs, particularly kelpies and kelpie-border collie crosses, sometimes with just a dash of blue heeler to give them more courage and keenness to find cattle.

There is a famous dog's grave on the cattle route to the Dargo Plains, at what was once the first camping site out from Cobungra Station on the Omeo high plains. The place is still shown on some maps as The Dog's Grave. Although the stories vary about the dog that is buried beneath it, it has been maintained for more than 120 years, and stands as a touching mark of respect to one particular man's dog and to every working dog in the high country.

On the way down from the plains, the steers and young

cows without calves often take the lead, followed by the cows with calves at their sides, and finally the older cows at the rear. The stockmen must keep the mob together and prevent it wandering off to graze. They use their stockwhips often and the sound can be heard throughout the muster, echoing across the plains and into the valleys like gunshot.

The huts of the Victorian high country are still often used, unlike those huts in New South Wales which are now rarely used for their original purpose. In the early days. tents were packed for shelter, but they were useless as protection in bad weather; so the stockmen began to build huts, both on the stock routes up to the plains, and on the runs themselves. It gave them a permanent roof over their heads in any weather, and somewhere to rest during long drives.

The huts were almost always built in sheltered positions, with an area nearby for holding the cattle, and access to water. Typically, they were about six metres by three, with a stone fireplace and a detached chimney at one end, to reduce the danger of fire. A sleeping platform stretched across the full width of the hut, on which four or five men could sleep, often head to toe.

Although many of the huts have disappeared, they are very hardy, withstanding the heat of the summer sun, the weight of snow sometimes for months on end through the winter, and the rain that rots the timbers. Bushfires are the huts' worst enemy, but they have saved many lives from fire, sometimes only after the occupants have soaked themselves and the walls of the hut with water.

Once all the cattle are in the yards and the drafting is complete, the business of branding and earmarking the cleanskins begins. Branding is a hard job and there is always the danger that an irate mother will come charging to the defence of her offspring, which results in a wild scramble for the safety of the fence by the stockmen.

The stockmen thrive on the companionship and the hardships of their life in the high country. There is many a bush poet among them and the poets they prefer are bushmen like themselves, who understand the dangers they face and their love of this beautiful place as Banjo Paterson did. Under the stars, with a blazing fire to warm them, they talk about their horses and their dogs and their heroes— usually men long gone, who came up to the plains as they have done. And they talk increasingly of their common foe, those who would turn them off their runs.

The leaseholders pay a fee to the government of about three dollars a head for the cattle they graze on the plains, regardless of the size of the run and this, together with the cost of getting the mob up on to the plains and back to the winter pasture, makes it not much more than a viable proposition.

The system under which the cattlemen hold their snow leases is positively antiquated and in many respects they are worse off than the New South Wales settlers in 1836! At least then they had 14 years' security and were compensated for any improvements if they were turned off their leases. Today, they have 12 month leases, which can be terminated at will by the government; and the only compensation they are given is the opportunity to remove their fences and huts at their own expense.

Over the century and a half that cattlemen have grazed the high plains, they have overcome just about every imaginable hazard that can confront a grazier. But now they face an adversary that may well prove insuperable, a very vocal body of opinion that believes in the concept of a contiguous national park stretching unbroken from Canberra to the outskirts of Melbourne, and a park in which there is no place for the cattlemen and their herds. Eleven of the 100 families have already been given notice to quit. It seems that an era may be coming to an end.

It is a complicated and highly emotive issue. The cattlemen argue that there is no serious damage, only slight change to an ecology which is now balanced with its use by people. It is their view that the much earlier and severe changes were the fault of rabbits and that the proliferation of weeds in the high country comes from a dozen other sources just as guilty as their cattle. They also claim that many of the accusations levelled at them are based on research carried out across the mountains in New South Wales on Kosciusko and the Main Range which has a more rigorous climate, is higher and has more exposed terrain and different rock types, soil and plants.

They argue that the leases that were terminated in New South Wales were being grazed by sheep, not cattle, and sheep put far more pressure on the land than cattle. They crop the grass much more closely, and selectively eat out

The Fitzgerald family make their yearly trek to the Bogong High Plains each summer, bringing the cattle back to the lower country before the cold weather sets in.

many of the herbs and grasses that are in greatest need of protection.

The risk of fire, which constantly haunts the cattlemen, has become a major issue in this highly fire-prone region of the world. Historically, the Victorian highlands were never deliberately burnt to the same extent as the Snowy Mountains, although the stockmen certainly did burn the spurs behind them as they came down in late autumn, maintaining that it cleared the floor of dead wood and scrub, improving the grazing for the following spring, and created essential firebreaks.

The cattlemen claim that the closing of the Kosciusko National Park to all grazing (often quoted as a model for what is to happen in Victoria) and the end of most protective burning, has created an ecological time-bomb. This is a highly political issue, and the cattlemens' lobby has become increasingly active. When 300 horsemen rode through the streets of Melbourne to deliver a petition at Parliament House, a huge crowd lined the streets to cheer them on. More recently, 400 horsemen rode to a protest rally on the Bogong high plains. Demonstrations like these are drawing attention to the cattlemens' concerns.

Banjo Paterson's High Country

It is an odd role for the cattlemen and not one they relish. Under the stars with a blazing fire to warm them, these people know they face their greatest challenge yet. Perhaps 150 years of tradition do not count for very much any more. Perhaps it doesn't matter in the overall scheme of things that an irreplaceable chapter in Australia's history may be coming to an end. But no matter what the rights or wrongs of either cause, it will be a sad day indeed if these fearless, independent cattlemen have to bring down their mobs for the last time.

Chris Stoney winning the coveted Cattlemens Cup at an annual mountain muster.

Postscript

It is easy to lament that the high country has changed, that it is no longer the forbidding, lovely place that Banjo Paterson understood so well. True, most of the cattlemen have gone and already the legendary horsemen who rode the half-inch hanging tracks along the mountain side have drifted into Australian folklore. Even the winter snow is not half so deep.

But little has altered. These lovely, treacherous mountains are no different, one moment warm and enticing, the next wild and bleak. Ferocious storms tear across the peaks, bending the gnarled snow gums before them. The deep ravines are just as black, the great amphitheatre of the mountains' western face no less magnificent.

Cockatoos still screech their ghostly warning as they fly blindly through the snowstorms and the sweet perfumed Alpine marsh-marigolds miraculously open, even while they are buried by the snow. The winter streams still tumble over icy rocks and the little mountain lakes and tarns remain unchanged. Whole mountains still are carpeted in snow daisies, so dense that one might think it winter again, the flowers deep drifts of snow.

It is impossible to read Paterson without feeling the ghosts of those who were here before. The extraordinary and courageous men and women who, with no conception of where their journey would take them, set out to open up this forbidding country—the Pendergasts and Campbells, the Faithfulls and Treasures. It is hard to walk through these hills and not experience the sensation that one is sharing them with the half-mad shepherds, alone for months on end with only their sheep for company; with the ticket–of–leave men and the bushrangers; or with the miners at Kiandra, enduring the terrible winter and the wet freezing fog that blanketed the hills each morning in their frantic scramble for payable gold.

These things will never change. The high country of Banjo Paterson remains the high country of every Australian.

Index of photographs